To

Maurice

Best Wishes

JANUARY RIVER

An Irish woman views the pacification of Rio de Janeiro's notorious favelas in preparation for the city's world events.

Marie Byrne.

GW00578577

www.mariebyrnenow.com
email: mbnowinternational@yahoo.com

www.fast-print.net/store.php

JANUARY RIVER
Copyright © Marie Byrne 2014

A catalogue record for this book is available from the British Library

ISBN 978-178456-051-5

First published 2014 by
FASTPRINT PUBLISHING
Peterborough, England.

CONTENTS

4

Information about the Author

Marie Byrne was born in a rural part of Co. Meath in Ireland. Her father passed away suddenly when she was eleven years of age. Marie would cite this as influencing her belief that if you want to do something now is the time – it is the only time we can live in – not the past or the future - just now. As her mother took on the responsibilities for running a small farm and family Marie grew up unhindered by gender job labelling. 'As my father was gone his jobs fell on my mother's shoulders – a case of do it yourself or it does not get done. My father was a much older parent when I was born so a closer link to major changes in Ireland's history was afforded me. As a youth he lived through its civil war - the Michael Collins and Eamon de Velera era.' Marie is intolerant of injustice.

Following her time working in a junior school Marie continued her journey exploring the possibilities of change and the challenges people face daily. For the greater part of her life she has worked in the field of drugs, alcohol, related issues of crime and social disintegration.

Marie believes it is possible to create more caring communities – starting with us first.

Marie completed her studies at the University of Kent at Canterbury following training in the US on Drug Prevention. She continues to train and increase her knowledge on how people can live to their full potential. Marie has been working internationally for many years and has seen the effects on communities worldwide from emotional pain, drugs and alcohol misuse. Travelling to the furthest regions of Australia, the favelas of Rio de Janeiro and areas rich with culture has given her a broad scope on problems affecting people generally. The Australian government and other countries representatives have consulted with Marie Byrne on National policy.

She is founder of the award winning charity Aisling Group International-Marie has learned at the coalface the effects of national drug policies on growth or reduction of drug problems in our countries today.

She is a regular guest on international, national and regional written and spoken media where she is well known for her candid interviews. Following her work in Australia she was invited to be a Director of Parent-to-Parent Australia. Marie has lived intermittently in Stockholm in Sweden – a country for which she holds a great love. She is impressed by what Sweden did to improve its social and environmental care system. Marie sees there are sadly some of the usual pressures emerging to get Sweden to fall in line on drug policy with the rest of Europe that chose harm reduction. Not a good idea she believes. Marie has addressed the North/South Inter Parliamentary Association (Northern Ireland & Republic of Ireland members) in Parliamentary Buildings, Stormont, Belfast, and Northern Ireland on the issue of drug/alcohol misuse and its consequences to communities worldwide. Marie believes her years involved in various sports are also a factor in getting her to try out new ideas and develop projects. She later became President of the Irish Olympic Handball Association following her run as a member of the Irish team. She remains international representative for Ireland to the World Championships. Marie was involved with the first Irish teams to take part in this event. She believes everything can be achieved but it is difficult to do it alone. "Relevant others have played a major role in all that I have worked on or achieved to date.

I am grateful to have friends, family and people who care about me. These are the ones who help my ideas become real and make life a happier place by far."

ACKNOWLEDGEMENTS

There are always people who help create adventures and projects. I couldn't have mine without them. All those who helped bring me along the way, family and friends too many to name. They know who they are. The trials and tribulations of life all teach their lessons, I am grateful for them.

Laura and Maria are the greatest achievement of all. Projects pale in comparison. They are the stars that shine brightly for me. A good team.

Sincere thanks are due to the police who risk their lives in Rio and Ireland in the line of duty every day. They helped me understand the complexities of this beautiful region. I am indebted to my friend Lieutenant Colonel Victor de Souza Yunes for inspiring me to visit Rio de Janeiro and form an objective opinion about this city.

Thanks also to the following police officers for their help, Colonel Alberto Pinheiro Neto, Lieutenant Colonel Cândido Joseli, Lieutenant Colonel Edson Duarte dos Santos Junior and hospital director Colonel Sandinha. My thanks to policewoman Elaine Ferreira for her patience, pride in her city, fun and help. My helpful contact Carlos for good directions. I am especially thankful to the favela residents and people of Rio who welcomed my intrusions.

Louise Ferriter, journalist, researcher and so much more, for helping so kindly in reviewing my ramblings in the middle of her busy days. Thanks Louise for doing so without fuss. You kept me going.

8

The late Jim Cumberton, his wife Peggy and John Ralph deserve recognition for lighting the road to recovery for so many. People are alive today because of their care. To save a life is priceless. They never 'said the right words' just the truth! We need more like them. Lindsey Pennycook, one of the first to make me see the possibilities in life, just believe! A good friend. My Swedish 'family' Christina and Peo, home from home, Börje Dahl and numerous Swedish friends. They taught me a lot about what can be achieved with kindness, help, belief in yourself and good support. Eamon Keane, friends do matter. PJ Nolan for his encouragement.

Childhood memories shared with Rosie and Terry. Former Assistant Garda Commissioner Kevin Carty, we need more like him- always supportive.

He has the know-how, tenacity and ability to make the difference – one of a kind. Glad to know him. Former Assistant Garda Commissioner Kevin Ludlow – helpful and supportive over the years.
These officers supported training in the past for those in need. To the members of the programs I worked in, still living or deceased, I learned so much from your lives and resilience. I appreciate all that I have been given.

Thanks to Emmet O'Dea for his consideration, discussions and quest in life. Same Pod.

Time to get my motorbike for the next adventure. The answers lie within us all. Happy searching. Big hugs everyone!
    Marie Byrne

Editing: Louise Ferriter, Journalist
Photographs layout: Laura Flynn
Cover; www.badapplefilms.com

FOREWORD

In 1994 Sweden became a member of the European Union. The year after that I was invited to the EU parliament in Brussels to attend a drug political hearing. At that time I worked as a drug political coordinator in the county of Örebro. I was, and still am, a firm believer in the restrictive drug policy we developed in Sweden following a time of drug liberal experiments gone awry in the late sixties.

I remember how shocked I was hearing distinguished members of the EU talking about just reducing the harm caused by drugs – harm reduction policy. Working harder with prevention, early detection of abuse, and drug free recovery for people suffering from addiction was not as high on their list.
For me this sounded like words of resignation.

The time came for questions from the audience - a woman from Ireland raised her voice. A member of the parliament had just expressed she had no problem at all that her own children smoked cannabis, "as it is a 'soft drug' - not nearly as dangerous as alcohol, and far from the horrors caused by heroin".

The Irish woman said that it was very interesting listening to a politician talking like the addicts she regularly worked with, and finished by asking the EU parliament member if she was smoking pot.
The silence that fell in the auditorium was palpable. The lame reply from the member of the parliament was just embarrassing.

One can imagine that the Irish woman would have been content with this revelation of drug liberal ignorance in the headquarters of high ranking European politicians. She was not. She went on confronting them with her deep insights and very articulate arguments – leaving them speechless.

I clapped my hands the hardest that I could for her. Afterwards I introduced myself, and told her how much I liked her standpoint and her courage.

This was the first time I met Marie Byrne. For me Marie is a fusion of Joan of Arc and Rosa Parks. Though probably with a rougher sense of humour. Since then we have remained friends. Not warriors waging a war against drugs but internationally merely trying in our individual ways to protect future generations from the horrendous fall out of drug abuse. Marie's knowledge, street credibility and integrity are expressed in her writings - 'January River' ake Rio de Janeiro.
Börje Dahl (Counselor & Drug Information Specialist - Sweden)

INTRODUCTION

This book was conceived during long walks through the favelas of Rio de Janeiro. Truth be known, it has also grown from working in the field of addiction, drugs and related crime over many years. Working internationally has set the stage enabling me to see how underlying agendas are played out. The results affect communities on a global scale. My life's journey has been evolving in the process. Rio just set the spark alight to write about what I saw. The favelas are shantytowns, districts that until now have been cited among the most violent in the world. My intention was to visit Rio, meet a long-time friend and write a short article about the trip. That was before I realised the richness of this city's culture, mystique, unimaginable beauty and warmth of its people.

The level of criminality, gangs and violence to date cannot be ignored as the eyes of the global media focuses on the coming major international sporting events and beyond. It would be an insult to what Rio now represents were I to condense what I learned in two paragraphs. The beginnings, history of this city and its favelas are what great movies are made from and have been. I've included some of my day-to-day movements in Rio de Janeiro and some free time is excluded. Even more surprising are the parallels between Rio and Ireland that naturally emerge as I become more familiar with its make-up.

I met some of the most interesting and resilient people along the way – all have a story. I engage with people from Rio wanting to discuss their city with me.

These residents live in the favelas, in the city centre, or close to the famous beaches of Copacabana, Ipanema, Leblon and further afield. They come from every socio economic divide and from a diverse range of jobs.

My regular liaisons with the police responsible for safeguarding this environment sheds a new light on the challenges they face to do so effectively for everyone. I have sought through my research and subsequent discoveries to show snapshots of the complexities faced by humans in our countries today. This is a time when money is being made without conscience from the pain and suffering of others. This has only served to make me more determined to make information about prevention available to everyone. I continue to catalogue these suggestions for my next book, which is nearing completion at last. Writing has been a new challenge for me but that is what life is about, learning all the time and growing. It is time to get something of what I have learned out there in the public arena. What will be will be! Drugs have polluted and muddied the waters as greed for power and economic supremacy takes first place to caring for our fellow citizens.

I ask is there hope? I remain forever the optimist!

Marie

Rio de Janeiro

Microwaving and decapitation are the sports of the drug lords and militia who have ruled the poor areas of Rio de Janeiro for decades. Now as the world's eyes focus on the sports of the Olympics and the World Cup due to take place in this vibrant city, Rio is expected to deal with its violence.

Breath-taking beaches like the Copacabana and Ipanema attract huge numbers of carefree tourists who line up to visit the famous landmark of Christ the Redeemer. However residents in the favelas or slum areas have waited for their redeemer to rid them of lives gripped by fear and hopelessness.

Rio has seen some children live a harsh existence in extreme poverty. Many have turned to prostitution, begging or stealing as a way to survive. Sniffing glue and using drugs dulls the pain – but not indefinitely.

The church of Our Lady of Candelaria became a landmark following the deaths of eight street youths. Shot dead by six people on July of 1993, some of these shooters were off duty police; the young people's deaths are still remembered. Death squads emerged in the disillusionment of a struggling society. Mistrust grew between civilians and police. The law enforcers who stood for justice were to suffer in an environment where the public now viewed all with suspicion and contempt.

This is a city that has seen busloads of people set alight in the past, by drug gangs, as calculated havoc took its toll on the streets.

On December 28th 2006 in Rio de Janeiro, on the poorer north side, the drug gangs who set alight buses also opened fire on police stations leaving 19 people dead and injuring 21. Others carried the scars in the aftermath.

Two policemen and seven people burned to death in one of six torched buses. According to reports, gang members used handguns, machine guns and grenades in 12 attacks on police stations and outposts. It was suggested the drug gangs' were 'flexing their muscles' as a political representative took up his new post. Advance warning derived from police intelligence said gangs were planning these attacks.

Police action was seen as having prevented the situation from getting much worse.

A policeman lost his life in the up market Lagoa district and a woman was killed during an attack on a police booth in the Botafogo area.

Similar acts took place in São Paulo leaving a trail of destruction in its wake.

Murder and torture have been a regular occurrence

- Conscience to criminals' means weakness and only the strong survive!

I have worked in the field of drug and alcohol prevention and misuse for 25 years. In the beginning I was somewhat uneducated to the full extent of drug related corruption and use. I may have started out a bit young and innocent but it has been a long journey. I have watched people across continents fight hard to gain back control in their lives and communities from the scourge of drugs. On this path I have developed my views on life and the world. Drugs have a cost - both monetary and human. They are one of the biggest threats to humanity. I've worked internationally with government and non-government agencies but most importantly with people at ground level. All are looking for help to overcome their fears and pain. We all are! I continue to seek out support for prevention and care for those suffering the effects of drugs, alcohol – and the subsequent fallout. I've seen how these substances are used to camouflage personal pain - temporarily. The pockets of the corrupt and greedy that prey on the suffering of others are lined with blood money. Corruption spreads its tentacles into the highest echelons of power and some business environs to serve the few. The poor and hurting are dragged ever deeper into a quagmire of despair. I've asked myself is it worth making the effort to change it? – You bet it is! Can we succeed? Yes!

Lieutenant Colonel Yunes in the PMERJ military police is the inspiration for my wishing to visit Rio de Janeiro, albeit a delayed intention first formed when I met him many years ago in Sweden.

At that time we were both attending an international event on drug and alcohol problems and solutions. The Lieutenant quietly made his own mark with his deep understanding of the complexity of the drug trade. He acknowledged the vulnerability of humans. He had a genuine pride in his country and the city of Rio de Janeiro.

The Lieutenant has a 'good heart', as they say a genuine consideration for others and a desire to do what is best within his capabilities.

At the conference, we discussed various social issues. We concluded that we all had similar views on the destruction caused to our communities by drug and alcohol problems.

Borders did not matter; the fall-out from using these substances is the same. The Lieutenant is a great ambassador for Rio and one who genuinely wants to make a difference. The seed was sown. I decided at that point I must go and see Rio and its hidden depths. It has taken longer than expected but never too late.

Over the years I followed how the violence of the shantytowns better known as favelas, developed in the city of Rio de Janeiro – its reputation for beauty and criminality spread globally. Shanty-towns have grown notoriously in areas of extreme poverty including countries such as South

Africa. In some districts in South Africa devices have been fitted in cars to reduce theft. They are capable of severing limbs as the accelerator is pressed - such is the value of life. Brasil and any country where the plight of people has gone unheeded with poor social support services are breeding grounds for instability. Some will see only one way out – through drugs, weapons and crime. Poor areas I realise should not be criminalised as many inhabitants are not involved in crime but must endure an existence where it is affordable to live.

Ireland also has seen an increase in destructive behaviour. Unprecedented violence has risen akin to that seen in Brasil where drug use was allowed to grow. Decapitation and burning is not exclusive to Rio's favelas. It has also been played out in Ireland today and Europe throughout time given certain conditions. It is not a geographical problem but a human one. It is a warning of how desensitised people can become to barbarity if social issues are left unattended. How we learn to justify any act, are uncaring towards others and unaccountable for our actions demands answers.
Award-winning journalist Tim Lopes was a former favela resident. As a child he lived in the Mangueira favela.

Favela residents approached him for help in highlighting their problems. They claimed the drug lords had started prostituting young people and making them perform sexual acts, orgies in public. This took place at the 'baile funk' gatherings where Brasilian music beats out across the favela. People dance, some teenagers and adults use drugs and public sexual activity is a possibility.
Lopes had previously covered stories from the favelas about drug trafficking. He carried a hidden camera to discreetly photograph criminal activity.

Gun wielding gang members were at the music event as usual. AK47s are a popular choice of weapon here, even with the teenagers involved with gangs. These guns can cost today, between US$ 6,000 to US$9,000. Rocket launchers are now part of the arms cache available to drug gangs. They have sometimes been better armed than police.

Unfortunately Tim Lopes was discovered on this investigation in the favela Vila Cruzeiro.

Notorious head drug lord Elias Pereira da Silva abducted Tim in July 2002. Elias's nickname was Elias Maluco. Elias Maluco means "Madman Elias" or "Crazy Elias".

During his ordeal, Lopes was subjected to unthinkable torture. He was pistol whipped, shot in the feet and blinded by a cigarette.

One of those present later said that the father and husband pleaded for his life.

Following a fake trial, Maluco sentenced him to death.

Lopes was brought to the top of another favela ruled by criminal gang law. As his hands, legs and arms were being cut off, residents could hear his screams but they were too afraid to intervene.

The tortured journalist was placed in the centre of stacked rubber tyres and saturated with diesel fuel before the unthinkable: he was set alight. The horrific but common practice in the favelas or with criminals is called micro-onda or microwaving and has also been used to kill policemen who have tried to apply the law in the drug dens.

Some charred fragments and badly decomposed remains later identified him in a secret cemetery for victims at the top of the Favela da Grota. DNA testing confirmed it was indeed Lopes. Other remains interred here are often of rival gang members, former lovers and young girls.

Lopes' charred camera and watch were found - the only reminders of a world where there is no time but the present and no promise of a future.

Maluco and 6 other men, who participated in the murder that night were later captured, charged with his murder and sent to prison. Their sentences ranged from 9 to 28 years.

Eliseu Felicio de Souza who set fire to Lopes was sentenced to 23 years in jail and escaped on a visit out of prison in 2007. De Souza was later seen armed and dealing crack openly in his old territory, favela (shantytown) of Morro de Alemão. He was rearrested when police raided the favelas in 2010.

Claudino dos Santos Coelho, sentenced to 23 years and six months, escaped with other criminals from Bangu prison in February 2013. Police intercepted Claudino and many other heavily armed gang members in September 2013: he died in the gun battle that followed.

Ângelo Ferreira da Silva was sentenced to nine years in 2005. He got a lesser sentence as he cooperated and named everyone involved in the murder. da Silva escaped from prison on work release but was rearrested in 2010 at his mother's house.

Elias Pereira da Silva (Maluco), leader of the notorious Comando Vermelho gang who instigated and gave the orders to murder Tim Lopes was captured in "Operation Choke". After a fifty hour siege he was arrested in the Favela da Grota in Complexo do Alemão and sentenced to 28.5 years in Bangu prison. He was later transferred to another Federal prison following street disturbances in which nineteen people died when a bus was burned and police stations attacked in 2006. In 2011 he was sent to the Federal Prison in Campo Grande, Mato Grosso do Sul after another wave of street violence that intelligence police said was ordered by Elias (Maluco) from prison. In order to intercept any criminal maneuverings, police constantly monitor the links between prisoners and street drug gangs.

In the favelas, horror stories abound of hands severed from robbers as a lesson to others and the tale of a police officer that met a gruesome death after running out of petrol at the entrance to a favela.

It's common here for children as young as 10 years of age to be recruited by drug mafia as lookouts and drug dealers. Children often have no chance - they learn to torture and murder under the influence of drugs, supplied on a constant basis by their drug bosses as a form of control.

I wondered how such a level of hatred and fear among the youth has been cultivated. This did not happen overnight and I wanted to find out why and if, at all possible, this culture could be changed.

This type of brutality is what gave Rio one of the worst reputations in the world for crime. Is it a Rio problem only? Or is this violence insidious, creeping into any so called civil society given the right components? If the answer is yes to the latter then I believe it is possible to identify these elements and prevent or counteract the vicious destruction of a caring society. Rio's highlighted problems taking all the attention may be a distraction from our own communities that are seeing increased suffering and crime. Are the efforts of police and authorities here in Rio now making a big difference? –This is very exciting if they are.

In Ireland we too saw the death of a crime reporter, journalist Veronica Guerin, shot to death as she stopped in her car at traffic lights in the city of Dublin on the 26th of June 1996. A mother and wife she met her fate at the request of those who made their living from drugs. The very effective Criminal Assets Bureau was born following this cruel murder and has seized millions of Euros worth of assets from Irish criminals. It is likened to the days of Al Capone who evaded prison for mobster activity until he finally was charged with a crime – discrepancies in his tax accounts. Sadly people still think it's cool to say they 'just snort a little coke at parties or using cannabis/hash doesn't harm anyone'. There are drug gangs in Ireland making millions from the brisk business provided by the Irish. We all have a responsibility in reducing the proceeds of the fat cats.

October 30th - The Plan

I was about to experience Rio de Janeiro, the second biggest city in Brasil in South America.
Over 202,507,013 million people live in Brasil, which is home to the second longest river in the world - the Amazon. The magnificent waterway accounts for about one-fifth of the world's total river flow. Rio de Janeiro was the capital of Brasil until Brasilla took over the title in 1960. Rio still continues to thrive despite the change and has been thrust into the limelight as the host of two of the world's premier sporting events - the football World Cup in 2014 and the Olympics in 2016.

I plan to travel to Rio to see how the city is combating its crime problem, especially ahead of the arrival of the world's top athletes.
I want to see if it is as beautiful and yet unsafe as I have heard.
There is an expectation on the city to dispel any fears for safety if it wants to attract visitors. It must secure some of the most dangerous areas in the world - the favelas - in order to ensure total safety at the coming world sports events.
Ironically it was in a Brasilian favela that one of the greatest footballers of all time hailed.
Pelé is not noted for his background but rather his talent that secured him a place in the record books as the footballer

to score the final goal in injury time to see Brasil win the 1958 World Cup final.

2014 will be Brasil's second time to host this competition, the last being in 1950. This time the world's eyes are on the city yet again where new goal-line technology will debut on a World Cup stage - but will the same scrutiny be applied to scores chalked-up in the favelas?

Going for Gold in Olympics and World Cup

The first stage of planning for the World Cup started in 2009. High-priority and long-term infrastructure projects included stadiums, airports, ports and urban transport at a cost of R\$ 24 billion (approximately US\$ 15 billion).

Three million Brasilian tourists from other regions and 600,000 international guests are expected to descend on the city.

The Ministry of Sports said that in a recent survey it is forecasted the 2014 World Cup could generate R\$ 183 billion (approx. US\$ 117 billion) in economic activity for Brasil.

Projected figures of 700,000 direct and indirect new jobs are proposed as part of this forecast.

As the World Cup 2014 passes, Brasil can turn its attention to hosting the 2016 Olympics before counting the costs of the pop-up businesses and projects that deflate post-event.

It will be interesting to see how these multi-million venues and projects pan out post 2016.

Rio de Janeiro will be the first South American city to host the Olympics and only the third to claim the role in the Southern Hemisphere.

By the time it begins there will be approximately 30 competition venues generally in the Barra da Tijuca area, which is seen as a nice part of Rio. There are three other places in Rio where events will run - Copacabana, Deodoro, and Maracanã. The famous Maracanã stadium is now upgraded before the World Cup.

As I thought about all the attention to detail that these huge events demand, I wondered how Brasil would safeguard those attending.

My life-long work in the field of drug, alcohol misuse, prevention and related crime nationally and internationally has taught me that people can change their behaviour. We can change but it takes commitment, effective strategies and different choices.

Our life's direction depends on our choices. Any assumption that we are powerless in designing our destiny and must accept whatever is thrown at us – is inaccurate.

Choices that create change for the better are exciting and give hope. We cannot alter everything but we always can decide how we react or respond to any given situation.

Ralph Waldo Emerson said, 'We cannot teach anyone but we can create the environment where they learn the truth for themselves'.

Questions I want answered!
   o how can people change their life for the better, regardless of any personal problems?
   o how do some people achieve what appears impossible?
   o how can a community, city or country operate more effectively and take care of its occupants?
   o what is the catalyst that makes people take action to deal with crippling corruption, greed and suffering?
   o how can attitudes develop to enable people to make choices that will benefit both them and their community?
   o what overall effects come from nurturing small

children and instilling values, confidence and hope?
o how can people overcome their limiting beliefs?
o what is the benefit of changing their destructive lifestyles or communities?

I want to see how Rio is tackling serious issues and how effective are their efforts. Spending time in this famous city will give me some opportunities to assess if there is any improvement.

The responsibility for clearing up the crime problem predominantly falls on the shoulders of the Rio de Janeiro military police. They are better known as the PMERJ police. To get the job done, requires well-planned operations and forays into the toughest regions of the city, I am to discover.

A short flight to Heathrow in London and on to Rio de Janeiro. Arriving at Rio airport I am met by my old friend Lieutenant Colonel Yunes.

It is nice to see his trusted face appear at the airport. I am travelling alone and unsure of what to expect on arrival or what lies ahead.

My apartment is situated in the beautiful area of Botafogo. Property prices have risen here and I can already see why.

It has everything, views of the famous mountains, Christ the Redeemer, the water, beach, and a route along the water's edge for running, walking or cycling.

One of Rio's football clubs has its home here, Botafogo.

I am looking forward to moving into a city that has long intrigued me.

Portuguese explorers arrived here in January 1502 and called the area Rio de Janeiro meaning 'JANUARY RIVER'. Other Europeans followed suit making their home in this beautiful and unchartered part of the world. The main language is Portuguese. Some of Rio's natives are called 'carioca' meaning 'white man's home' from a Tupi Indian word. There is a city centre metro station named 'carioca' after them. Other people of African descent may be called 'Afro-Brasilian. Over three million African slaves were brought to Rio and sold on, during slavery, to work in coffee, sugar plantations and gold mines.

Favela Origins

Brasil was the last country to abolish slavery in the Western Hemisphere in 1888. It was from this period that links to the earliest favela communities have been made. This was the time when black slaves with nowhere else to go settled in Rio de Janeiro. Now free, they had no rights to work and accommodation was not available to them.

Historically the first favela originated in Brasil in 1897.
Another influence around this period was the return of 20,000 troops to Rio de Janeiro who found themselves homeless and without financial or government support. These troops had fought and won the deadliest civil war in Brasilian history, the War of Canudos (1893-1897) against Antonio Conselheiro in Bahia. A nearby hill called Gamboa was then taken over by the soldiers where they built small shanty homes. This place became known as Morro da Favela (the hill of the favela.) The word 'favela' originally was a 'skin irritating tree' in the spurge family that grew on Gamboa. 'Morro' means crown shaped hill.
The film 'Cidade de Deus' (City of God) based in Rio de Janeiro shows the rise of one man as leader in the favela. It is fictional, but close to the truth of how the criminal gangs developed their drugs and arms trades and forged links with some corrupt public representatives in the process.
Brasil emerged from its military dictatorship that lasted from

March 1964 to March 1985 – poverty was rife. It was the 1970s that the favelas we know today in Rio began to evolve. During this period there was an increase of immigrants from poor rural areas of Brasil such as São Paulo.

The availability of jobs, especially in the construction sector in Rio attracted those trying to build a better life.

Drug dealing in the favelas began with cannabis/marijuana. It was the 1980s that brought a major influx of cocaine from Colombia and Bolivia. It changed the way of life in the favelas forever. Drug use increased - the arms trade developed. AK-47s, Eastern European, arrived from Paraguay. Behaviour and attitudes changed and so began the reign of criminal gangs and militia.

Brasil has gained the reputation of coming second to the US for its cocaine use. Only on the playing fields would coming this far up the league table be acceptable.

One of the biggest cocaine trails begins in Colombia run by the Colombian cartels and makes its way across Panama and South America. Colombia's close proximity to Rio de Janeiro makes it an obvious market place for this destructive drug. Making money from drug sales attracts some young people who want to climb out of poverty and see it as a means. It involves others who do not use drugs but allow greed to navigate their business interests.

Comando Vermelho (Portuguese for Red Command) is a Brasilian politico criminal organization. It too has its own rival gangs. It was founded in 1979 in the prison Cândido Mendes. Ordinary criminals, met with left-wing political prisoners there. They were members of the Falange Vermelha (Red Phalanx). From this union a gang was formed. The notorious criminal gang Red Command is still active and involves young people with the lure of drugs, weapons and power. It is a typical way for terrorist or criminal gangs to recruit - the promise of importance and power to the marginalised. The Falange Vermelha had fought the military dictatorship. CV (Comando Vermelho) can be seen written in some favelas as a territorial mark.

Great things have come from Rio de Janeiro too. It is home to the 125-foot (38 meters) famous statue of Christ the Redeemer. It is set on top of the Corcovado granite mountain peak as it rises 2329 feet (710 meters) above the city. Corcovado generally means 'likened to hunchback'. I plan on seeing it up close. The famous monument has a link with Ireland in recent years as it glows a neat shade of green for St. Patrick's Day, March 17th. – part of Ireland's push for tourism in Brasil.

Brasil and football are intertwined. Pelé, real name Edson Arantes do Nascimento who started playing football in the slums is one of the all-time greats. Other talents who hailed from Rio include Ronaldo whose real name is Ronaldo Luis Nazario de Lima. Ronaldo's name appears on the list of greatest footballers better known as FIFA 100, compiled by Pelé. Ronaldo has also won the FIFA player of the year three times.

Ronaldinho, real name Ronaldo de Assis Moreira is another famous Brasilian footballer. Kaka, real name Santos Leite started playing at a local club and to progress to the major leagues. After AC Milan, he was bought by Real Madrid for US$89 million.

In Rio, football gives hopes and dreams to countless children caught in a country of both great wealth and dire poverty.

Botafogo is a safe base to work from, I am reliably informed. The Lieutenant's friend, Alex, suggested this place. Alex remembers a time when Rio was an even better and safer place to grow up, despite some poverty. Children, he said, played on the streets and people walked about freely without fear of attack. He proudly speaks of his upbringing in this city. The Lieutenant introduced me to Alex some time ago.

As someone who has lived overseas in America, for a long period he can help with information for my visit. He is always a very nice, straight talking person who says what he thinks on any given topic. If you ask him for advice he will paint a clear picture for you and then you must decide the route of action yourself. As a professional photographer normally based in the US he has taken photos of some very famous and distinguished personalities. His eye for technique and the use of light is amazing. Photos taken by him in Rio are spectacular involving its natural beauty, shading and colour.

Sadly some months ago Alex became very ill and due to a number of complications had both his legs amputated below the knees. He is still very ill in hospital. We must all wait and see how he responds. Normally he stands six foot two and has multiple black belts in martial arts. I feel sad such a nice person has this challenge but everything has a reason and I hope he survives this ordeal. It hangs in the balance just now. There is limited visitation for him. I will wait and see when is appropriate if at all, to do so. Getting better is more important.

I guess I'll have to wait and see if Botafogo is as safe as he reckons. For my part, I intend to proceed with caution until I become more confident in my surroundings. Kidnapping here can happen and I have to take that seriously on board.

I have no idea what to expect but I am open to finding out what is the real Rio de Janeiro. This is not just a tourist visit!

31st October

After my first night in Rio, I settle into my apartment before deciding to check out the city. The apartment is very spacious and suitable for a number of people. So this is ample room for me. The multi bolted entrance door gives a sense of home and safety. The bedroom is bright and airy with a window overlooking the streets and facing Christ The Redeemer. There is a sitting room and kitchen with all the usual mod cons. There is a reminder to cover plastic objects in direct sunlight.

The side window faces the apartment closely located across a laneway. I can see directly into their family apartment as they relax in front of television, shoes off, shorts and t-shirts on. I must remember to pull my blinds when indoors. The majority of TV programmes are in Portuguese and a few of them are sub titled. Thankfully there is the desired air-conditioning in each room. It can be very hot in Rio. The added blinds keep out the midday sun ensuring a nicely cooled space. The apartment is on the sixth floor of a well-kept older residential building in the centre of Botafogo, within walking distance of all amenities. People living in this block are residents of the city who live and work here. The front lobby is wide with a high ceiling allowing light through its long windows. Green plantation takes up one corner. Having security men at the front door reception desk is welcome. Nothing gets past their attention I can see. Courteous and smiling they maintain safety in the building, which is a relief. It has not gone unnoticed to them who my first visitors are.

The Lieutenant greets me at the entrance to the apartment block and is accompanied by a Major from the PMERJ police also. My friend wants to check what I am interested in seeing and to liaise with me when needed. They will assist in any way they can so I can get the most from my visit here. A police officer has been assigned to help as a translator when the need arises – that will be invaluable to me. There is great encouragement for me to see what is now happening in the present Rio. This openness is refreshing and encouraging. I would like also to travel on my own to experience for myself what the city holds. I understand they are concerned for my welfare at all times. Obviously to see the real Rio I must do it alone as much as possible but not be too foolhardy.

There are places too dangerous to travel in unless you have security present.

We begin my stay with a trip to police headquarters (HQ) through heavy traffic. So the Irish M50 is not the only road with tailbacks!

HQ is based in the centre of Rio de Janeiro's main business and shopping area. There are around 46,000 police in Rio so this is the hub of operations at all levels. The current General Commander is Colonel Erir Costa Ribeiro Filho.

HQ is a very busy place with the weight of responsibility for clearing the crime problems in Rio squarely placed on those within its confines. There are considered formalities and salutes as a variety of police personnel meet or greet each other within the compound. Officers pay respect to each other's rank. I too am receiving the occasional salute, which seems very respectful if not a little confusing initially. Still I could get used to this. Armed police are stationed at HQ entrances and you must have permission to enter.

As well asspecialised units, HQ contains an internal police department to try and keep the force free from corruption - an issue that has demanded attention if confidence in the police is now to grow.

The lead officers of the PMERJ police are based on various levels of HQ, around an open-air walkway. Colonel Pinheiro Neto is the Chief of General Operations, Colonel Robson Rodrigues da Silva is the Chief of General Administration, my friend Lieutenant Colonel Yunes is Secretary of the General Staff at this time and Lieutenant Colonel Cândido is the current Commander of Battalion policing in tourist areas. Policing decisions for the World Cup and Olympics will be made from here and the results will be their responsibility. This is a daunting task with global media attention focused directly on their every move.

The hot weather is glorious in comparison to what I left behind in Ireland. I have shrugged off the winter clothes and donned bright coloured summer wear. I love the freedom of movement in lighter clothing. Thankfully water is always in good supply here to combat the dehydration that can be caused by the constant heat.

Lieutenant Colonel Yunes tells me about the structure of the PMERJ military police and plans for the future. At this time he is Secretary of the General Staff, one of the highest positions in the police.

Though they are called military police they are not army personnel. In principle, the Brasilian Constitution designates Brasilian military police as a reserve force of the Army. In practice they remain separate. PMERJ are seen as a police organisation.

They use the rank system of military such as Lieutenant, Captain and Colonel. Officers of this rank normally have become educated to a high standard in third level education. This is possible to achieve in the police force here. The State Government politically appoints the General Commander of the PMERJ police.

In Ireland too, the Garda (police) Commissioner is also a political appointee. He is responsible to the Minister for Justice, Equality & Law Reform, who in turn is accountable to the Dáil (Government). Obviously with this manner of selection in any country there are pros and cons that depend on the process being fair and honest. Any political corruption could spread into the police if it is misused.

With this manner of selecting there is the possibility that an officer could be chosen on his or her political connections rather than being the best leader. It is important that this does not happen both for the morale of the hardworking police and in order to build trust with the public.

Lieutenant Colonel Yunes takes his role in the police very seriously and knows the value of a good working relationship with his fellow officers and those under his care. He is known to work well with his staff - a skill not possessed by everyone.

His passion and awareness of social issues and policing has not changed since I first met him years ago. If anything he is more experienced, professional and acutely knowledgeable now. Lieutenant Yunes is a former member of the famous Choque battalion from 1991 until 1995 and has added to his experience over the years since. He is very well versed on the urban warfare associated with Rio and the favelas.

The Choque battalion of Special Forces - Choque is a military police organization of the Military Police of Rio de Janeiro. The focus is to control riots and civil disturbances in open and closed areas to safeguard people, among other activities.

Lieutenant Yunes has honed his experience and developed his policing in order to provide the best possible outcomes. The Lieutenant acknowledges that military police work hard to make areas safer. There is, of course, the human element of corruption that can be considered by some. This must be dealt with - corruption is not something he will tolerate.

Lieutenant Junior is next door and has time for a conversation about how Rio is preparing for the World Cup and Olympics. He also is involved in the preparations. Lieutenant Junior is fluent in English and so describes well the effort they are putting into reclaiming the favelas from the drug barons. He will study previous Olympic Stadia and safety in his preparations over the coming period.

Lieutenant Yunes is a busy man but makes time to help me as I plan a general itinerary for travelling in Rio. The plan is flexible and open for changes, that way I can take any new opportunities to experience the area fully as they arise. He encourages me to check out the city for myself and come to my final conclusions. I intend doing just that. I like to discover the truth of any situation, if I can. He suggests I assess what is happening in Rio. He has not tried to influence my observations or commented on the powers that be. The Lieutenant thinks I must see for myself what happens here. I like his attitude and openness as I would like to decide if it is improving or not by what is reflected at ground level. All these officers are well educated and have a good knowledge of Europe and international policing.

It makes the exchanges and discussions, informative and very interesting. Lieutenant Yunes is always good to talk to. His approach to his work is humane and caring. The Lieutenant is acutely aware that communities want to feel safe and functioning well and he strives to support them as best he can. He has a tendency to humbly play down his achievements. He plays a pivotal role and takes his responsibilities very seriously. As always his infectious laugh over some minor matter sets everyone off. Behind the fun is a very observant, strong and likable personality. He is most definitely someone you would want to have on your team in any given situation.

BOPE POLICE

The Lieutenant has arranged for me to meet Colonel Pinheiro Neto. Time to see what 'the boss' is like.

Colonel Pinheiro Neto was Commander of the famous

'BOPE' police, (Batalhão de Operações Policiais Especiais). Translated to English this means 'Special Policial Operations Battalion'. He has earned the right to wear the famous badge of 'BOPE'.

Renowned as one of the toughest units in the world, BOPE police deal with urban warfare, terrorism and operations in the favelas. They also work overseas on missions. BOPE's origins date back to 1978. Police are invited from other units to train for the BOPE but the majority will not make the final grade due to the challenging selection process. There is an over 95% failure rate and it is said the unit cannot be corrupted. Corrupt police will not be tolerated within the BOPE police unit. BOPE police are doggedly persistent in accomplishing their tasks or operations and are not easily thwarted.

BOPE police Badge; "Faca na Caveira" (Portuguese for "Knife In The Skull"), The BOPE police, motto and logo.

The badge consists of the "Faca na Caveira" (Portuguese for "Knife In The Skull"), BOPE logo and motto. The badge or symbol is made up of a skull flanked by crossed knife and pistols. The knife and pistols symbolise the most basic police weapons, while the skull represents death. The two weapons flanked on the skull means the BOPE victory over death. BOPE police can be superstitious about the badge and believe it helps protect them when they are out on operations. One policeman's life was saved when a bullet hit his badge, a story, which fuels the belief even further.

It will be interesting to speak with the former Commander of this unit.

The Colonel's time is taken up with his position now as Chief of General Operations so it is great to get this opportunity to meet with him. He is very actively involved in running these very important missions in Rio. Media covering this police work in here regularly interview the Colonel. A straight talker, the Colonel explains what the challenges are for the police in the coming years. I can understand his views on human poverty and the care that is needed for people to live with some quality of life. To eradicate crime these are serious considerations to take into account. It is not just a police problem but requires help from all aspects of society address the needs of those most vulnerable.

The Colonel describes the situation as 'complex'. There are different issues to be tackled.

I have seen over the years political groups move in to poor areas. This helped them in some cases to gain a foothold while appearing to be there solely to help the underprivileged. Their only motive was to gain votes in an upcoming election. People of low means used as pawns in a political game. This political manoeuvering complicates and hinders work that could help those most in need.

The world's media is focused on the World Cup and Olympics but it is the Catholic Pope's visit, at this time that would place heavy demands on their operational skills Colonel Pinheiro Neto points out. The new Argentinean Pope, attracting a major influx of people vying to see him, in the city, over a short period of time requires a well-organised plan of action. Brasil is predominantly a Christian country. Roman Catholicism has the highest number of followers despite a decrease in recent years. A visit such as this is a big challenge in a city with six million people and a lot of traffic, but one that he knows is manageable.

Plans for large events include all security measures. The Colonel works hard to facilitate the numbers coming to the already crowded streets of Rio de Janeiro in order to facilitate smooth running and safety of those in attendance. Events such as this can be a stage for opportunistic gangs or campaigners to get media attention globally. Police are deployed to relevant strategic positions and a plan of action put in place for security. Heavy work time traffic and busy public transport are always a consideration to alleviate pressure on the city I'm told.

Apart from all the high profile gatherings due over the coming years having services to help people on a day-to-day basis is a challenge worth tackling anyway in the new Rio he believes.

The Colonel mentions how the World Cup and Olympics are being taken very seriously. Given resources they will now be able to make positive changes in reducing crime in Rio. It will take time to change the criminal areas to law-abiding communities but according to the Colonel, it is happening.

Lieutenant Cândido and Lieutenant Yunes also sit in on this meeting. Lieutenant Cândido, another officer with a warm personality, is responsible for police at all the famous landmarks in Rio and is also involved in security for the events. He has fluent English, which helps with more technical discussions. It is best not to underestimate this officer who has also served in the 'Choque' armed police unit. These police are tough and specially trained to deal with very serious riots or threats to communities. Riot control here is complex where others with hidden agendas may blend with the more peaceful crowds. This can escalate an already emotive march into public disorder.

The officers present are capable of making important decisions under pressure and must be decisive and honest in their leadership. Reaching the rank of Lieutenant and higher is a major achievement in itself in Rio and there are a small number who are in that honoured position.

Portuguese is the language of Rio and English is less spoken than I expected. Those who can speak are a little shy initially to say anything but when relaxed will surprise you with their understanding. So after a time English is spoken by all three, a big help to me in gaining accurate information.

The Colonel and I talked about the problems Rio faces with poverty and drugs. Colonel Pinheiro Neto highlights the need to help families experiencing drug problems. 'This is a story that needs to be told', he says. Focusing on the family is very important to him.

He feels that support and help should be easily accessible to parents when drug abuse is in the early stages in their home. He believes this could help solve the problem before it takes a grip on the person, the family and the community.

He knows that drug abuse doesn't stop with the one person - it escalates to harm those around the individual and the wider community with disastrous consequences.

I couldn't agree more! I inform him that the lack of similar services in Ireland is creating the same difficulties. I understand exactly what he describes. I have seen it too many times in Ireland and other countries. I and others have lobbied long and hard for support that could alleviate the suffering before it grows into a bigger problem. Sometimes it falls on deaf ears. Opportunities have been lost to intervene at an earlier point in substance misuse and social problems and look at the wider implications. Ultimately the chance to save everyone time, money, heartache and loss of life are sadly missed. I have never understood how people and social issues must take a back seat to materialism. In the end the cost to society of ignoring the problem far outweighs the benefits in any capacity. No one is immune from the fallout from the break-down of our communities. We may live on an island but no man is an island.

This compassion for others from a police officer is not what some might initially expect if they are to believe all they hear about police in Rio. The police have been accused of corruption. There was a lot of serious criminal activity among a number of law enforcers and their connections. Low salaries and morale led some to choose involvement in illegal activities. Extreme force has been condemned where others believe less is best.

These officers present are at pains to point out that police corruption was in the past and they do not want it in their present - they are adamant that it will not be supported under their command. Whether it is totally eradicated or not remains to be seen. The intent to have an accountable and effective police force is high on their list. They are unwilling to tolerate corruption and criminality among their own troops. My instinct allows me to feel comfortable working with these officers.

Media has been highly critical at times and many police I talk with feel some of the coverage is unfair and needs a more balanced approach. Police I speak to, who want to do a good job are hurt that people could assume they are all corrupt. They are deeply offended that some may say they don't care about those they serve with their lives. There have been many deaths in the line of duty over the years, in the police. The coverage, they feel, is causing a public mistrust in general and is benefitting the criminals. As I recall how drug money has bought many over the years I expect there may be some in media who have also benefited from this lucrative trade at the expense of others. It is not uncommon in any country to hear a media outlet is sometimes supportive of a political group.

In my own experience, selling newspapers does not always

involve investigating to find the truth. It can depend on who owns the media in question.

Information could be censored in some cases by those who benefit from doing so. Monopolies on media were supposed to be eradicated but is it really gone? It appears money sadly buys those with only their own interests at heart and can breed corruption at any level. I am open-minded and compile my own, hopefully educated views on Rio.

Corruption in the police is mentioned in a general way. Indiscriminate generalisations do nothing to encourage those who are honest. Working with serious crime for low pay in very difficult conditions is not very satisfactory. For some it appears media forget police live in the communities with their own families. Media has played an important role when reporting responsibly, professionally and with sufficient investigation on issues. Responsible reporting is to be encouraged.

Of course any corruption within the police must be tackled. Without doubt there have been cases of laziness, misuse of power and unwarranted brutality by some police. Arrests have been made. It has to be stamped out if communities are ever to work together to eradicate criminal activity through trust, co-operation and action.

Wealth and poverty are back to back in Rio. It would be great to see investment in people less well- off and their needs. The Colonel is correct in his thinking in my opinion. Increasing the resources for these people and investing in relieving their plight is also very important for the safeguarding of Rio for the long term.

Pacification

The Colonel explains how the police are systematically

reclaiming the worst favelas from the notoriously violent criminal gangs. As the BOPE police reclaim the areas, the UPP police follow. They move in, establish permanent bases within the favelas and monitor activities. UPP stands for Unit of the Pacification Police (In Portuguese, Unidade de Polícia Pacificadora).

Their role is to maintain peace on the streets in favelas that are newly reclaimed from drug traffickers and militiamen. At this time there are approximately 26 UPP police units already established in favelas. By the end of 2014 they are expected to increase to 45. That is a very big undertaking but whoever believed that 26 would already be in place? - Yet they are.

The UPP police form a relationship with the communities of the favelas to work together in order to keep people safe. This is about building trust and being effective in their job. A mammoth task I can imagine, though wonderful if it works. I shall see.

These police operations into the favelas have been likened to UN peace missions with three steps, demobilize, disarmament and integration.

I've seen reports that Rio's government is investing $15 million to help police train at the Police Academy. It is proposed that by 2016, they will increase the force to 60 thousand police officers in the state from its present 46,000.

To put this in perspective Ireland for example has approximately 13,366 police (Gardaí). In difficult economic times, the government in Ireland stopped training new recruits in recent years in an effort to save money. In 2014 it's expected the training college will re-open on a limited basis. Even then it will take a number of years before the new recruits are trained.

Garda Síochána na hÉireann translated means "Guardians of the Peace of Ireland"; more often referred to as the Gardaí

("Guardians") and is the police force of Ireland.

The money given to increase police personnel here in Rio is seen as investment in the long term through a reduction of crime. The state of Rio includes 43.696,054 km² and the Head Quarters of the PMERJ military police is based in the city of Rio de Janeiro. The PMERJ police motto is 'to serve and protect'. They have a presence in every city of the state of Rio de Janeiro.

In Ireland, with one of the highest rates of drug and alcohol misuse in Europe, a reduction of police numbers occurred through the ban on recruitment and members reaching retirement age. This is at a time when police (Gardaí) are needed more than ever - even for a street presence! A reduction of police many years ago in Rio too, is seen as one of the decisions that contributed to the growth of criminality and drug trafficking.

Selected Garda stations in Ireland have closed nationwide as a cost-saving initiative. Many dedicated Gardaí are now forced to use private cars and phones on duty. This too can make it easy for criminals to trace where they or their families live, leading to safety risks.

Making policing more efficient is a wonderful idea, but it appears the strategy in this case is the opposite of what is working elsewhere efficiently. Different working conditions will play a part in how the new police respond in their roles. Sweden too reduced much of its criminal activity when it invested resources into a number of key areas as Rio is now doing. Sweden learned that closing its police training college for a number of years was not good for security overall and it has now reopened. It would be wonderful if police were not necessary to safeguard communities. Until people fully internalize and consider the welfare of their fellow man as well as themselves it seems we must rely on the assistance of law enforcement to supervise our behaviours.

In recently reclaimed favelas police carry heavy-duty weaponry that is necessary, they tell me, as criminals are still a major risk in the early days of PMERJ police occupancy.

The gangs started to take over completely in the 1980s and lawlessness developed. This growth happened under various governments. A lack of political-will to commit the necessary resources needed to solve the social difficulties in the favelas didn't help.

I later hear a politician on the radio in Rio suggesting disarming police, making them friendlier looking, and less threatening in appearance. I do not advocate gun use generally. The brutality possible in criminally run favelas and the cruelty man can bestow on other human beings would deem it utterly irresponsible for police in this case to work unarmed in such dangerous conditions. Criminals who dismember and burn people alive don't really care if the police look friendly – less armed they are just an easier target in a hostile environment!

In the favelas, cildren have been forced to shoot dead their friends. In 2009 drug gang members in Morro de Macaco favela shot down a police helicopter. This is what the police and all of Rio are up against!

In reclaimed favelas such as Santa Marta, which was given back to the people four years ago, police now carry more discreet pistols. To reduce their firepower is a gradual process.

The favelas run by criminals have urban warfare and their problems are complex. Urban warfare is not just about a small argument on the street but involves rounds of ammunition. In this case the war zone happens to be local communities' of Rio. Vicious armed drug gangs will show no mercy if you enter their territory uninvited or upset them and it doesn't take much to do that. Feuds between rival criminal gangs with equally savage results are part of this warfare. Fuelled by drugs, hell can break loose with dire consequences. No one is safe in this environment where life is cheap. Reclaiming the favelas is an interesting and necessary strategy in reducing problems overall it seems.

Colonel Pinheiro Neto tells me how well the reclaimed favelas are progressing because of the efforts now being made to control the violence and criminality. It can and is being done, the officers enthusiastically point out and I am looking forward to seeing what this means exactly.

A lot could have changed before now in Rio I imagine concerning its rise in crime. As with all troubled areas I've seen internationally, as long as trouble appears to be controlled in some quarter of a city those involved will be left to their own devices.

That is until the problems spill out into the general population and political power is forced to address the issues. There are many questions as to why such brutality has evolved. Corruption is never far away from the answers. Authorities are not blind; they can see people need help. Nevertheless the present is all any of us ever have, and the work has now begun. This is a great time to watch how a city may evolve from its harsh beginnings.

About 3,000 police took part in a large-scale operation, which included tanks, helicopters and weapons in pacifying Rocinha favela. It is seen as a successful mission without violent conflict and death.

Colonel Pinheiro Neto was the commanding officer of the BOPE police at that time. He is keen to point out that he is not confined to his desk and plays a hands-on-role in major operations.

His mental and physical strength have me in no doubt that this is the case.

The Colonel has a direct, grounded and deep understanding of the problems in the favelas. He talks not just about control but also about all the human tragedies that occur.

He speaks of the poverty and its effects on communities and how it creates difficult conditions for people. I can identify with his sentiments, having watched the deterioration of drug/alcohol problems in Ireland over many years and a lack of will from government bodies to address them with long-term effective plans.
It's frustrating to see that these bodies of power realise their schemes are not working but continue to implement them regardless.
It's terrible to watch apathy and hopelessness grow in these families as they learn to think no one cares about them or wants to help them change their circumstances.

I have seen the untold generosity of others when they want to help those less fortunate. Former Assistant Garda Commissioner Kevin Carty, a George Cross medal recipient, comes to mind. He understood the value of supporting ordinary people in their efforts to prevent their children from misusing substances. His efforts played a major role in making the help Colonel Pinheiro Neto spoke of, available to parents.
I recall all the well-attended training groups and enthusiastic participants.
The Assistant Commissioner has since been sought internationally for his experience, knowledge and commitment to what is just. His work in the highest echelons of policing has benefited countries overseas. Nevertheless it is our sad loss, as Ireland needs more personnel of his ilk. That is if we are serious about gaining back control of our drug problems and save lives. Unfortunately in the field of drugs and alcohol misuse I

believe corruption, ignorance, misconceptions and a wish for anonymity has sadly given those who could help an excuse not to.

A teenage boy sits outside the city centre church door. The strain etched on his face of living each day in poverty and fear. His eyes alert to passers-by. He has such a nice looking face. His hair has grown long and is now a slightly knotted Afro style. His attire is a couple of sizes too big for him. I can imagine how he could look if he was not so hungry looking, cleaner and better dressed. It's frustrating to watch and wonder what can be done to help.

The Colonel's honest directness may have upset the powers that be in the past and some might say softening the message would be helpful.

Some can get their message across more tactfully than others. Perhaps tact would help - but more honesty from those in positions of power would be better. The scenario reminds me of the actor Jack Nicholson when he played the part of a Marine Colonel, in the movie 'A Few Good Men'. His justification for covering up wrongdoings was that others "just can't handle the truth."

Often hiding or ignoring the truth because of fear is just as misleading as lying. Sometimes the idea that the end justifies the means can be dangerous. Lobbying for change has led me to different realisations.

I remember being told on a number of occasions over the years by officials, 'just say the right words and you will get what you need' in relation to seeking financial support.

In Ireland, pretending all is well when it's not has been a huge part of our problems. Too many people have been left vulnerable. People have become suicidal because the powerful failed to instil confidence in their ability to decrease the misery experienced by those in need. Dishonesty is a method used to camouflage all is not well in a country – and a need to be liked is not a good enough reason to avoid truth even when it is painful. Omitting to tell the truth is another form of avoidance and dishonesty. Honesty at least lends to finding solutions. It's a platform where trust can build.

"The only thing necessary for the triumph of evil is for good men to do nothing." This is a quote attributed to Edmund Burke delivering a speech in England's House of Commons in 1770. It is equally true today.
Working in tough policing conditions in Rio is not for the faint hearted and often brings the threat of death - but thousands of police ignore the danger to stop the triumph of evil!

BOPE police give advance warning before entering a favela during pacification missions in the hope that the criminals will leave before gunfire must start and innocents are killed in the crossfire.
It's a strategy 'to save lives' rather than all out warfare in the favelas. The BOPE police deal with urban warfare as part of their brief and shoot-outs are not uncommon between well-armed gangs and the BOPE unit. This elite group of trained personnel must clear the way for UPP police. Burning tyres at the entrance to favelas and boulders blocking the narrow streets are warnings of traps where they can lose their lives carrying out such a task.

When Rocinha favela was taken over by the BOPE police and the UPP police units established there, the next operation was to clear over 450 tons of rubbish, the Colonel explains. Up to then no waste collection service would dare to enter the favela to remove the decaying waste. This was a feeding ground for vermin including rats. The rats in favelas are very big especially at close quarters – not the petite things we see scurrying around in Ireland – oh no, much bigger.

Crime bosses running the neighbourhood ensured free electricity and no taxes in the favela in order to curry favour with residents. Many of the poor stayed in the favelas because of this. Some might argue that giving taxes from drug sales is the way to go in order to help people. I have little tolerance for the debate anymore.

The favelas use of drug money is a warning as to how badly that affects everyone in the long term. Drug gangs put some of the money from their illicit proceeds back into the favelas where the intricate maze of dangerous illegal electrical, internet and television cables are maintained – residents did not have to pay at least not with money but at times with their lives. Rio's version of 'affordable housing' as we know it.

Despite the murders, drug running, arms trade and fear, they could see that financially they were better off staying - Better the devil you know than the one you don't comes to mind!

The Colonel tells me there are over 6 million people living in the city and approximately 2 million of them live in favelas. He mentions how the issues affecting these areas are very complex. Interestingly the population of the island of Ireland is close to that of Rio. There are 6.4 million people living in the Republic and Northern Ireland. Not a big difference in the numbers except one is a city and the other a country. Brasil was run by a dictatorship and Ireland had problems under England's rule that led to some very historic battles for freedom.

The slum areas in Rio later grew into the present day favelas, as their difficult living conditions were ignored. Today's problems have gradually grown from neglect over time. A lesson other countries could learn from. Ireland could take note of how ignoring growing community issues breeds more lethal attitudes - and unhealthy societal norms. The provision of social services and support is a necessity not a luxury. Chaos develops in places where hopelessness reigns.

The tentacles of crime and violence made their way out to the wider city.

It's difficult to understand how youths can be responsible for such violence and savagery. These young people have been born into very difficult circumstances and become victims also to their harsh environment. If all you ever know from childhood is pain, fear, crime and a mistrust of everyone, it's easy to see how extreme choices are made. You do what you have to do to survive in this world where there are no boundaries. There are no rules, no barriers and consciences.

The cleaning up continues in Rocinha favela.

I can understand the frustration by those who wanted to make changes but were denied support. There are similar problems in all countries where I worked and no less in my own country, Ireland. It is frustrating to see this lack of will to invest resources that could turn problems around.

This apathy towards change deprives young people of the care and help they crave and the advice and direction they long for.

November 1st - Police Hospital

Another sunny day in Rio, but then again it is warm here all year round. This is spring and temperatures fluctuate between 26 and 40 degrees. My feet are not fitting so well in my shoes due to heat expansion. So it's off down to my local shopping mall that is several floors high. There is a vast array of shoes. A gentleman tells me so much beef is exported from Brasil they have plenty of leather for all types of footwear. Sandals are good quality. I purchase a pair of flat shoes.

The fashion here seems to be flip-flops, but I wonder how people walk long distances in them? I plan to walk a lot. This is a great place to exercise.

At my apartment I meet the female policewoman who is helping me with translations. Her name is Elaine and she commutes a four-hour round trip to work each day. She is generally based in the popular tourist areas such as 'Christ The Redeemer' Corcovado and other areas overseas visitors frequent.

Elaine leaves home early to catch the buses to work. Travelling with me she can also practice her English - a good arrangement for both of us. She may end up with an Irish-Brasilian accent. Spare the thought! It is difficult otherwise for her to get the time she needs to master the language fully so this will be a good opportunity to learn more. English as a second language certainly opens up other possibilities in Brasil just now. I've arranged to use some recommended and reliable local transport. They will ferry me to the appointments and my out of town destinations as needed.

First we visit the Military Police Hospital and meet with the Director Col. Sérgio Sandinha Celméd. Lieutenant Yunes also joins us as a former Director of the Hospital and he too is aware of its needs. Respect and comradeship is noticeable between the two men in their responsible roles.

The present director Colonel Sandinha is a surgeon. The challenge as director is managing all the administration that goes with such a responsibility. As a surgeon he was not working in administration in the past but now it is expected of him. Further development in administration is needed to run departments smoothly and efficiently I muse.

Col. Sandinha and his staff are passionate about their work. I can see how frustrating it is for them trying to give the best possible service. It is obvious that more investment will allow for improved services. The staff is hopeful this will change in the near future. Funding for the hospital comes from the State and National Government but with the pressures on the services in a city as busy as this, it appears to me getting this in order is urgent.

The five main issues presenting at the Police Hospital, I'm told, are hypertension, diabetes, obesity, alcohol/drugs and cardiac problems.

So far I have noticed a lot more people seriously obese than I had expected. Fast food is readily available and availed of. Obesity it seems due to easy fast and processed food is now a huge problem almost worldwide.

Addiction Recovery Programme - Police

Easy access to drugs and high stress levels are a potent combination! It's no wonder then that some members of the Rio police have alcohol or drug problems and addiction. These issues further impact on their family and work if left unchecked. Although similar issues exist in police forces throughout the world, it's not often that the problems are admitted or addressed at top level, as is the case here.

The Rio de Janeiro addiction recovery program is a mature way of dealing with a common problem in society, regardless of socio economic divides.

It is heartening to see the staff developing strategies to help their comrades. In this programme those addicted learn how to shed their feelings of fear, shame and destructive behaviours to become well again. It is not easy to be a police officer with an addiction, especially in Rio where police are in charge of weapons. Some police find it difficult to disclose what they perceive as shameful weakness when normally they are seen as the protectors. It is only when these men and women understand how it takes courage to face their fears and change that participation in the programme is easier to establish.

The recovery program is drug-free and provides a residential detoxification unit for those coming off drugs.

They then have access to counselling and group therapy in a residential setting within the hospital. This program was set up initially during Lieutenant Yunes's term as director. He seemed to realise that addressing these issues and offering support makes the police more secure and disciplined in the long- term.

Police using illegal drugs or misusing alcohol are compromised in their job. In buying their supplies illegally from drug suppliers, they are immediately open to blackmail, extortion and endless other difficulties to keep their 'dirty' secret.

This program tackles any addiction problems within the force and offers professional help and care for the addicted police and their families – everyone benefits!

I have long-advocated random independent drug testing for police, members of An Garda Siochana (Irish police) or any police for that matter. I believe prevention and early intervention is essential.

Police not misusing drugs or alcohol have nothing to fear from these tests and help should be at hand for anyone that fails the random exam. It is a test that already exists in some countries.

The overall opinion is that drug testing in the police could also act as a deterrent. An officer in Rio says at present they have a system in place to deal with suspected misuse of substances but drug tests could be a consideration.

The most misused drugs by police in the Rio program are marijuana, alcohol, cocaine, crack and ecstasy. Stress is a big problem for police who often find solace in heavy drinking.

Surprisingly heroin is a bigger problem in Ireland where there are approximately 10,000 heroin addicts on methadone (synthetic opiate) in the capital city of Dublin alone, which has a total population of over 1,110,627million - the city and suburbs covers an area of 317.5 kilometres.

Methadone is a substitute for heroin, costs Ireland millions of euro and I believe has not helped reduce drug use in Ireland.

Especially when you consider what methadone actually is. It is like legalisation by the back door I feel. I am not alone in my observations either.

This 10,000 is the tip of the iceberg. It does not account for all those on drugs such as cocaine, crack, ecstasy, cannabis, prescription medication, alcohol, synthetic substances and a host of other potions. It doesn't account for the remaining opiate or heroin users who have not presented to any drug recovery program. The lack of services to help addicts come off all substances is a scandal that will haunt Ireland into its future unless it acts now. The lack of provisions will leave a legacy of death and unnecessary suffering.

In Ireland, children are starting to experiment with substances at around 12 years of age and younger.

It is unfair to judge the adult too harshly without knowing the full story, as he was the child that the system or adults failed! Helping addicts gain control and take responsibility, now that is a different matter. It is the way forward and I impatiently wait for the day we put more emphasis on prevention and recovery. No one I ever met wanted to or believed they would become an alcoholic or an addict.

Methadone as a substitute for heroin is not seen of benefit here in Rio. Drug-free programmes which help people to get off drugs and live a healthier way is seen as the best choice. When the brain is clear from these substances then the work can begin to learn how to grow, love, accept and live the life that is possible.

I am delighted that Rio has learned the benefits of helping addicts in this way and hope Ireland will follow suit.

Ireland persists with harm reduction methods in a country consistently in the top group of European countries with serious drug and alcohol misuse levels. Over 22 million

Euros is spent on methadone treatment each year! Check
how many people become free from all drugs including the
substitute methadone in the long term and there are no
figures available. How much money is invested in drug free
programmes to help people off all drugs or alcohol and sadly
Ireland fails at the cost to society.
In Ireland addicts are maintained on methadone and vie for
approximately 200 residential drug-free recovery beds
available in the country.

About 40 residential in-patient beds, last I heard, for
detoxification from drugs, is not enough. How can it be?
Ireland will have to step up to the mark if it wishes to save its
youth and reduce drug related crime. Already Ireland has an
increase in gang related murders, violent attacks on the
public, rapes, robberies and anti-social related issues. These
acts are not just applicable to problem drug use. I reiterate
those on drugs do not all take part in crimes apart from
illegally buying the substances. I'm not minimising that act
either. Nevertheless becoming un-inhibited under the
influence is dangerous and can open the door to
uncontrolled or changed behaviour. Ireland wants tourists to
visit this lovely island famous for its seasonal shades of green
and predominantly good people. If you want tourists to
arrive they must feel safe, our reputation for violence is
growing. Irish people are also entitled to a safe environment
where they care for children and loved ones.

The police recovery program in Rio is based on the 12-step
abstinence model but unlike some countries, it is non-
religious. Families are encouraged to come in for counselling
and be a part of the recovery process - a sentiment I would
fully support when working with addiction. The program I
have been involved with for many years is based on the
therapeutic community drug-free model. It incorporates all

the influences around the person such as family, school, employment and the community.

Through various methods including counselling it supports the person gaining back control of their life and moving on.

Back to Police Head Quarters and lunch-time with Elaine and Lieutenant Yunes at a nearby pasta restaurant and time to catch up during his short break. Good priced and delicious food is served with the usual friendly smile and pizazz I like so much from the locals.

The afternoon allows for some time to visit the famous 'Christ the Redeemer' on the top of famous of Rio's attractions.

Elaine is based here as one of her tourist area assignments. Her commanding officers including Lieutenant Cándido have made is possible for her to help out on the occasions when I might need assistance. We catch the transport to our destination. The small red train trundles slowly up the 20-minute climb to the top. The train is filled with visitors to the area and Brasilians from other cities. We pass an old closed down hotel in the green plantation, I am told it was visited regularly in the past by the Brasilian football team.

After we master some steep steps, there it is rising high above us! This famous monument synonymous with Rio de Janeiro is an amazing feature on the landscape. Today the sun is trying to peep through but at this height it is cold and misty. After wandering around for a while trying to see the famous face more clearly high above us we decide to finish this visit. It is a bit cloudy and cool in the swirling mist so better to come back another day to see the spectacular scenery laid out below us.

I've now started to think of coffee as I travel but need to head back to the car, so no time for that. I realise later people here generally drink water and soft drinks as they perspire a lot in the heat. I on the other hand am not about to let go of an old habit, as Elaine is to discover on numerous travels with me!

Night-time is when I may want to travel more alone and I am somewhat apprehensive initially. I hear stories of kidnapping for ransom so I am careful about what areas to walk and never carry valuables with me. Kidnapping by criminals has been used to make extra money. I wish them luck with me.

2nd November - Time for A Walk

Today I am able to check out areas between Botafogo and Centro - main business and shopping area of Rio.

One thing to remember about Rio is the holidays. The 2nd of November is a Christian holiday and there are a number of these throughout the year. It is All Souls Day. This is a holiday weekend and the city centre shopping area is deserted except for the homeless and those visiting the restaurants. There are many homeless who sleep under the awnings of buildings for the shade provided at this time. Rio can be very hot with a rainy season too. When the shops are closed with shutters down, it changes the look of the area and makes it slightly more unwelcoming.

Normally, there are many police posted during the busy times but this is not the case at holidays or night-time when numbers are reduced here. Seeing streets lined with shuttered windows and homeless people is a bit intimidating at first. I am not used to this area but they are not causing any problems for me. Young boys can be seen along a stretch of road near the cathedral and some reportedly thieve from unsuspecting visitors and locals.

I find it best not to stay loitering around on my own for too long but to be in the busy streets where there are police posted. As a visitor to Rio I am more likely to attract attention even if it is just idle curiosity. Unfortunately, many who live day-to-day under financial pressure in cities must survive some way and Rio is no exception. Robbery at knifepoint can occur here to both tourists and locals alike. Ireland is not immune to such attacks either. It is a symptom of the times we now live in and one that requires alternative ways of reducing these threats.

People usually go to Copacabana or the other beach areas at holiday time with their families. Family is important here. Staffs in restaurants are very patient with small children. Many people I meet take their family commitments very seriously and want to take care of their children and relationships as best they can. Drugs or alcohol misuse disrupts that regardless of what country you live in. Walking from Botafogo to Rio Centro brings me past the Santa Teresa favela, now quite an exclusive looking area with stunning views from the top I hear. It is on the outskirts of the business area in the vicinity of Lapa viaduct, known for its bars and restaurants. Many locals frequent this part of the city at night. Around the corner drug dealing and using transpires as darkness falls. As in any city it is wise not to walk alone or in secluded areas unless you have knowledge of what happens close by.

I am more relaxed now and find I can chat with people in whatever bit of language is manageable, at cafes and in small shops. French is the second language I learned and I'm finding I can understand enough in Portuguese to get by. Communication doesn't always depend on words but it sure is helpful if you are fluent in the language of the country.

Brasilians are delighted if you say something good about their homeland. I note their sense of shyness and pride as I recall all my positive adventures so far.

Anyone I have so far met in Rio has shown nothing but genuine friendliness to me.

On a number of occasions when I overpaid even slightly, my

mistake was immediately pointed out and a refund given with a smile.

It's a pleasant walk past many small stalls selling costume jewellery, clothes and all manner of items on the way home. I've walked over 20 kilometres this evening and mingling with natives wearing brightly patterned clothes, lends me a sense of local life. There are always colours brightening even the dullest pavement. Loose fitting clothing is worn in these temperatures with open sandals or flip-flops. After walking so much and with expanding feet, I now completely understand why. It's not long before I capitulate and join the flip-flop brigade, remarkably comfortable new purchases, I sigh deeply with relief.

During the next couple of days walking I find shops and cafes that will become my regular haunts with pleasant owners, waiters and home cooked local delicacies at reasonable prices.

3rd November, Saturday
Visit Praia de Copacabana and Ipanema

It is five minutes by metro from my apartment to Copacabana and Botafogo station is outside my door. I am not sure what to expect. In no time I'm on the train and scanning faces discreetly to check for would-be attackers. My survival and paranoia mode is still at high alert. A lot of local people who live in the area and work in Copacabana are on the train and some eye me with mild curiosity. Blonde and white skinned I just don't blend in as much as I thought.

However, they are always friendly and accommodating whenever I'm in need of assistance or information. Both the train and station are so clean. This part of the city is host to many tourists and has good transport links. Unfortunately the metro does not extend to all the suburbs and tourist areas and it is hoped a few extra kilometres will be added onto the line in time. Despite my initial trepidations, I arrive in one piece unharmed, paranoia intact!

Buy a green coconut and they machete an opening in the top and insert a drinking straw giving access to a very nice cool drink on a hot day in Copacabana and all for a minimal fee.

Copacabana is a busy area at the weekend and is well equipped with lanes for cyclists, skate-boarders, walkers, runners and families pushing baby buggies. Cameras are strategically placed throughout the area and are monitored by police at the local base. I am due to visit there later in the week.

A stall owner brings his pop-up shop home with him. The usual friendly smile is given as I take the photo. It is common to see these stalls in Rio. People trying to make a living on Copacabana pull their heavy makeshift shops to work and home each evening. Hard labour. No weight lifting necessary when this is your job. Toned bodies drag the awkward loads to and from the tourist areas along the beaches daily. It is their way of making a living and a physique most strive for in gyms daily, is an unplanned result.

Now just off the main beaches of Copacabana and Ipanema. The PMERJ police are noticeable in these tourist areas. Crime has fallen in recent years.

Poverty is never far away and people collect drink cans to exchange for money in order to live.

I take a photo of a young man who is carrying a large bag of cans on his back. He is pleased I want to take his photo. He does not speak English but we understand each other. I sit at my café table and feel somewhat guilty that I am taking without giving. I go back to him and show his photo. He beams with pleasure. There is no one in a position to take his photograph in his life. Money is not available for such trivial things as cameras.

I offer him half of my portion of hot fries. There was too

much for me anyway. He silently and slowly eats each one from the paper napkin savouring the taste. He is very graceful in his movements. I can see the scarring on his stomach that looks like knife wounds. Poverty and drugs go together. Cannabis is used to escape daily hardship and pain but gives even more misery as the drug takes control. I remember the Colonel's comments on the effects of poverty on the people of Rio. It is not easy to get up in the morning and wonder where your next meal will come from.

On the young man's back are the indentations from carrying so many collected empty drink cans in a heavy sack day after day. On his right elbow and arm the flesh is laid bare from some other result of a hard life. It looks red raw, possibly infected and in need of immediate medical attention but this is not possible for him to afford. Brasilians tell me of their disappointment with the health care system that needs more investment and better structures they say. He finishes his food, waves, and smiles warmly and says goodbye in Portuguese. I find even in poverty there will be many who make me feel humble by their generosity of spirit and gracious manner. We have so much to be grateful for in life. This young man accepted the food intuitively knowing there was no bad ulterior motive on my behalf for giving the food.

In doing so we both benefited from this moment of trust in our exchange. I believe in the Western World we spend too much time striving to build empires of money and miss the importance of what life is about.

There is nothing wrong with money but how we hoard, use or waste it meaninglessly is questionable as others starve. It is beyond belief that as civilised people we can allow this to happen today and are able to justify it.

The contrast between the very poor and the affluent is very evident in the tourist areas. The roads are better and more wheelchair friendly here. Streets in Rio can tend to have uneven paving and people can unwittingly trip over a rough surface.

Many of the poor live in the favelas. Some work in wealthy homes to earn a living and provide for their children. Others resort to drugs and criminal activity. The introduction of the UPP police to the favelas is making a positive difference on these streets I'm told. The poor live on the bottom of the favela, poorer live above them and the poorest live at the top, one favela resident says. He moved there after the BOPE police took over the area and the UPP police unit set up their base in the favela where he now lives.

I talk to a young man who speaks fluent English - all learned from TV. He lives in a favela with his mother and works in the beach areas. Now as we chat he tells me he thinks the police are corrupt. He has no cause to think this, just suspicion. It is normal in the favelas and elsewhere to automatically mistrust the police, he says.

He moved to the favela because it was cheaper than living on the main thoroughfare of Copacabana.

The favela, he believes, is now a much safer place to live because of the police presence.

Trust is gradually building between the community and the police, he admits.

If criminal gangs or those who may be corrupt law enforcers are not tolerated there is a real hope for positive outcomes in the city of Rio he says.

The young man accuses the police of past corruption and collusion with criminals but he has no direct experience or proof of this.

Confused, I ask him why is he in the favela if he thinks all police are corrupt?

He explains he feels safer living where there is a greater

concentration of police - this favela. They are doing a good job here he reiterates. His comments are conflicting and not isolated. There is a simplistic generalisation about corruption in the police that gives a false impression of all these men and women. Perhaps, I consider, it is not just in Rio that this occurs. There seems to be a universal mistrust of people in uniforms who possess so much power over civilians.

Of course, corruption did and can still occur in the force but it's being stamped out. I get a strong feeling from the former head of the BOPE police, Colonel Pinheiro Neto and lieutenants that they will not accept any such behaviour. There is too much at stake, too much to lose. Those who are trustworthy also want this governance to protect the greater good.

There are problems to be dealt with in police circles, of course, but not all are corrupt. Many police work hard for the community. These days they are developing a pride in their uniform. I speak with many police who are unaware of the purpose of my visit to Rio lest it influence what they tell me. At all times they are helpful and approachable regardless of whether they speak English or not. On one occasion a policeman took out his phone to find a map in order to show me how to find a particular street. He must have spent all of 10minutes trying to help me and he spoke in Brasilian Portuguese throughout.

What then is the future for those living in these poorer slum areas? It is obvious that in order for long-term improvements to occur, support must now be introduced to provide education and training for the residents. It will open up so many new possibilities for them. This process has started. The selection of Rio for the World Cup and Olympics has been the leverage for this change. It was needed long before now but the political will seem to have been missing in the past. It needs to be activated fully in the present. It is paramount actions are taken to help Rio develop and move forward for everyone's sake.

Brasil's economy has improved, as generally, the rest of the world has slowed. It is in prime position for growth in every respect. People exercise on the beach all the time. I love the freedom to exercise outdoor afforded by such permanently good weather. In this case two bats and a ball are required for two players. The ball must be kept in play and not land – there is no bounce on sand. It's quite a strenuous sport and in 30 degrees plus heat not long before you get in better condition.

Rope walking between palm trees demands great balance.

Copacabana provides a home for some, under its palm trees. During the day drinking alcohol or sleeping under an old blanket on the ground is not a totally uncommon sight.

Further along the beach Forte de Copacabana, the old army museum offers relief from the sun. Placed at the end of Copacabana it has some of the most amazing views from its base. Cannons, now obsolete, face out over the glistening blue water. Basic army accommodation, weapons and radio equipment are on display - reminders that Rio also was under protection from invaders in its past. The Fort was built in 1914 and saw the Lieutenants' rebellion of 1922, which became known as one of the most dramatic times in the Brasilian army's history. The Fort is now open to visitors. The statue of Dorival Caymmi takes a jaunty position along the Copacabana beach attracting many who want to stand beside it and have photographs of their national celebrity. Dorival was a famous Brasilian singer, songwriter and painter, son of an Italian immigrant and Brasilian woman. He was married to a Brasilian singer called Stella Maris for sixty eight years and died in 2008 aged 94 years. He was linked with the beginning of Brasil's Bossa nova that literally means 'new trend' and is a lyrical mix of samba and jazz.

Caymmi also included political comments in his music about government corruption. He remained active most of his life and passed away at his home in Copacabana in Rio de Janeiro.

Time for home and I walk briskly back to my apartment which takes about 20 minutes. I pass a very up-market shopping centre with designer brands on display. This is aimed at a slightly more well off group of people.

Then again there are a lot of wealthy people living in Rio; otherwise there wouldn't be a need for it. Salaries are low for those working in the service industry. Police are paid much less than their European counterparts and may need sometimes to have another job in order to take care of their families. Their low pay in extremely difficult and sometimes thankless policing situations has been a factor for some to choose to resort to crime. Not an excuse I say, nevertheless for some it was the reason for their decisions.

6th November - Business As Usual

My transport arrives once again and it's off to police HQ where we meet up with Lieutenant Yunes and some of the staff who are working in this section. There are a lot less females in the police than males but more are joining. Everyone is busy taking care of the day's duties, calmly getting through each one. One officer tells me how she balances family life and work commitments. The Lieutenant is very encouraging to the staff here and others who come and go, as I sit and observe. The Lieutenant emphasises how effective and important his staff are in helping get the job done. He is full of praise for their work. Any issues related to police are being dealt with and consideration is given to every situation that comes before the relevant staff. The corruption of the past, once again, is not welcome in this area. Too many people were hurt and compromised by some crooked officers whose actions have tainted the work of all. These police work very closely together and under the Lieutenant's command are making every effort to efficiently get through the rising pile of documents that must be dealt with. He readily points out that the personnel working here are his arms and it is important they work well together as people. This office has important responsibilities and a lot of administration to boot. The stack of files all needing immediate attention takes up the Lieutenant's time just now. As Elaine and I buy water at the small kiosk in the yard below part of the Head Quarter's enclosure, we listen to the fun and banter between police who are relaxing on their breaks. This is an experience also for her. Her everyday duties do not normally bring her to the Head Quarters to meet commanding officers. Translating for me when required has put her in this unusual position where she gets to interact with any officers-in-charge that I meet. It is interesting to see how she responds. They are very courteous to her as expected and she responds in kind. As ranks are acknowledged in the military police it does take her time to relax and be more informal in her communications in the Head Quarters. She eventually succeeds. At all times she is respectful to her superior officers. Elaine does comment that my friends in the police are particularly nice to deal with. She is invited to join us on most occasions and she strives to carry out her involvement with my visit as professionally and responsibly as possible. There is a disciplined approach to organising my schedule.

In the course of the day, she records all appointments that involve liaising with the Lieutenant's office or police generally.

Later that evening, I go for my usual run near Botafogo. I

run about nine kilometres along the running track by the water. It eventually leads me up towards Copacabana. The trees along the street bend towards the water making a semi arch over the track where I run. This provides great shelter during the daytime from the heat of the ever- present sunshine.

It is a slightly cooler part of the day now and I have less to manoeuvre around en route. People are strolling along the pavement taking in the beautiful engagement of sky and sea. There are old chalk coloured buildings on one side, remnants from bygone days, blending with more modern architecture and a number of shops. I decide it's time to return, as the light is fading and follow the traffic lane. It's not the wisest decision as I discover I must negotiate around a junction at the bottom of a favela and I'm apprehensive passing through a street where men somewhat imbibed have positioned themselves. There is a lot more graffiti here. The black writing doesn't look as artistic as the colourful paintings I usually see adorning the walls. It doesn't feel like the best place to hang out for a chat so I continue my run until I am back in a more open area and then home.

When I work out how to rent one of the many street bicycles, I will try out the cycle-lanes. Rio has extensive routes designated for cycling and they're something I want to explore.

7th November - My Birthday

What a great place to be for my birthday, Rio de Janeiro. I hope all my birthdays are this interesting with caring friends. I always enjoy my birthdays because it is the one thing that is just mine and I'm grateful for another year. How I spend this day each year has become very personal and important to me. It is for me a landmark of change each time. I like to have something special to remember from the day. It is not a notch on a calendar where life is whittled away but an acknowledgement for me to remember to use my time wisely – and with meaning.

I have learned it can be helpful not to over analyse everything to the extent I forget to live now. So it is nice to mark the occasion by having lunch with my old and new friends in Rio followed by the favela visit.

I always reckoned this process of having a number was developed by card companies for profit and government departments to help account for each person numerically and without personal human touch. This I believe, can lead to derisory decisions, which benefit few and leave no accountability for any human fall out. If you start going there you might actually fit into some slot designed for you. Freedom.

Back to Police Headquarters and I am introduced to Carlos another policeman, very friendly – easy to understand despite not speaking English. I am meeting with the Lieutenant, a police comrade nicknamed Batman for his similarity to the hero and another who teaches kickboxing, all enjoy fun exchanges and camaraderie. Perfecting their skills in multiple martial art disciplines is common in the Rio police. In fact learning martial arts is a way of life for a lot of people here. Many I've met have black belts in a number of disciplines. It has taken a lot of training and commitment to reach the level they have. Brasil is known for its high level of expertise in this area. Some say it is also the home of MMA. Mixed martial arts (MMA) a full contact combat sport that allows the use of striking and grappling techniques, both standing and on the ground. MMA fights are shown regularly on television here. Police may need to use what they learn in self-defence skills and martial arts in the line of duty to protect them or indeed to apprehend criminals. Young people living on the streets may use knives in robberies and it is useful to have extra combat techniques when trying to disarm them.

We discuss the benefits of staying fit as a police officer and the demands on them to be able to stay in control of a dangerous situation at all costs. It can mean life or death.

Lieutenant Yunes is also a keen surfer and likes to get out on the waves as early as 6.30am. He says it helps him focus during work, improve his fitness levels and reduce work stress. It is an activity that he feels gives him great returns and one of his passions.

Lunch consists of Arabian food with many flavours. In Rio there is a wide range of food outlets to meet all culinary tastes. During lunch I am kindly presented with the cherished official Brasilian football top - in the right size - for my birthday. Now I must find an opportunity to wear this honoured top. It is such a nice thing to be given this gift here in Rio and I am touched the Lieutenant has made the effort for my birthday, considering how busy he is. I thank him profusely for remembering my day and for the gift. He smiles knowing I am very pleased with his present of time, consideration and revered iconic football top.

The Lieutenant has arranged for me to visit a favela today. I am intrigued to experience life inside one of the city's poorest areas in order to gain an insight into the associated crime and social problems. This I hope will allow me to have some concept of the difficulties faced by the residents and those in power with the responsibility of improving them in light of the forthcoming World sporting events. I want to see how some choose crime and others such as Pelé go on to become one of the most famous footballers alive today.

Rocinha Favela

Rocinha favela has a long history of poverty and crime. BOPE police took control of it from hardened criminal gangs on the 13th November 2011. There were supposed to be approximately seventy five thousand known residents in the favela officially but it is estimated the full total could be between 100,000 and 200,000. There are now 26 favelas reclaimed. There are over 760 favelas according to the 2010 census. In one area in the city of Rio, seven favelas have grown together to become one mass of box- like tiny homes on the sides of surrounding hills. A long arduous task lies ahead to retrieve peace in all the favelas.

Rocinha is generally seen as one of the largest and densely populated slums in Rio. Families live in extreme poverty. Their homes are small shanties that are all crammed together climbing high up on the hill overlooking the city. The buildings were sometimes built eight levels high, one on top of the other. All of this slum area is squeezed into a steep rough landscape of approximately 0.80 square miles. Most houses in Rocinha have basic sanitation, plumbing, and electricity. The maze of electrical wiring hangs low over the streets. It will take more than policing to develop this community and support for these people. Government aid in all aspects of social care is required to impact on the poverty experienced here. Co-ordination of these non-government organisations and agencies to achieve total effectiveness will be a major task. Nevertheless, plans are in place for professional programs, partnership and suitable policing to kick- start positive development. The idea is to legitimise the favelas and bring them into line with the rest of the city.

However, we've all heard those 'buzz' words before, which result in nothing being done. Still it is worth clarifying if this is happening here.

I've certainly become very bored at meetings in Ireland and elsewhere where 'the right words' were used to manipulate others into believing something useful was actually happening to help. It seems they were nothing more than smoke screens for inactivity but the summaries sure look good on paper. In fact expensive looking, dust covered booklets, reports and pamphlets lie dormant on desks like abandoned graves. We've become used to having the obligatory get-togethers under a variety of social problem banners facilitated by various government departments as part of their policy directives. A lot of amounts to nothing and the weary faces of those regularly attending are testament to their dissatisfaction with the process.

I prefer to spend my time on what works. Life is too short to waste idly at the behest of others on that which does not change substantially the suffering of those in our midst.

Drug misuse in Ireland has been getting worse and meaningless talk continues. It is time to change our national policy – time to implement strategies that help those afflicted from drug use and yes dare I say it poverty. This can be done through training, education, prevention, intervention and real care, which I believe will save, lives. It has been done in the past - we just need to copy some of the better methods used elsewhere and stop repeating old mistakes. Restrictions on drug use must continue despite the push by the legalisation movement.

Thankfully most people still understand the need for drugs to be illegal.
Here in Rio words must be followed by significant action if any of this is to amount to something worthwhile in the long

term. Too many people have suffered for too long needlessly and must now have this alleviated by action, not empty promises. With the eyes of the World focused on and expecting real change there can be no mirages.

My driver is stopped at the Rocinha favela entrance. UPP police are stationed there permanently and are keen to know what business we have there. I give them the relevant information, they contact the Major at the top of the favela and we are allowed to proceed. The Major is expecting me.
As we drive up the winding street I see the buildings are small and substandard. The roof is burned off one and the further up we drive the more precariously the buildings lean against each other. Yet visually it works in some odd way – an abstract tapestry of boxes. Wheelchair friendly the favela is not. I imagine elderly people become housebound unless transport is available. Navigating up and down steep broken steps and narrow lanes is a great athletic fete here. Without help the infirm could be stranded. I remember hearing about these areas many years ago and how no planning permission was needed to build homes on top of each other. There are no building regulations and none have been implemented so their reliability is quite precarious. Whole generations of families have built over each other. It is a fascinating place.

The ever-present graffiti adorns the walls. Graffiti can be seen throughout Rio. Some of it is quite artistic and colourful. It amazes me how it is placed on the highest and most difficult to reach places. It shows what can be achieved if you want it! It appears as if writing a story or comment in graffiti makes you relevant or heard in this vast and complex urban environment. Everything is a message in the same way tattoos are common on males and females. All have something to say when you get down to it.

Travelling in the car with darkened windows means I can photograph and view people closely without attracting too much attention. We continue up the long drive over rough cobbled narrow streets to our destination. Until recently you could be shot dead by the criminals, even for taking photographs in the favelas.

Today Major Edson Santos is there to meet me. He has been notified I will be arriving. The Major is also a former member of the elite BOPE police and has been part of the units who helped take over some of the favelas. Presently he is commander of the UPP police in Rocinha favela. The BOPE badge is proudly displayed on his uniform. He recalls how much criminality took place in these forsaken areas of Rio over the years.

The Major points to the new UPP police base. It is under construction as we speak. We go inside their temporary base where police are monitoring the favela through well-placed camera systems, which are sending back images from vantage points. Police are now placed within the favela permanently and will remain there.

As it is not so long since Rocinha was taken over by BOPE police, they still carry heavier weapons other than their standard Taurus pistols. It is early days and they are aware that there is still criminality in the community. It would be foolish to lay down their arms just yet.

I ask what effect if any he feels the presence of the UPP police in favelas is having in Rio generally. The Major explains that since they started to take over the favelas, crime is reducing. For example 26 police were killed in Rio in 2006 dealing with criminal activity compared to 5 in 2012. In São Paulo where they are experiencing the effects of drug gangs at a greater level, 92 police were killed in 2012. It is estimated the drug trade here alone before pacification was worth over US$450,000 per week. The drug gangs also have a major side-line business in phones and

pirated cable TV. These are very lucrative illegal businesses.
There is an overall decrease in crime in Rio since the changes in the favelas. It seems to me to be a very good reason to continue with this work. I've been told two robberies take place daily, less than 90 per month, on Copacabana and the beach areas, since UPP police started pacifying the favelas. In such a densely populated area this is a dramatic change from previous years. The Major is adamant that they will continue to build relationships within the favela communities. Working together is the only way forward, he says, and will have benefits for everyone. He adds that the police are taking the upcoming sporting events very seriously and preparations are ongoing.

Of course more resources will mean better opportunities for residents of the favelas. Projects involving young people in sporting activities have increased and are helping to break down barriers between groups and police.
I am aware I am a little brightly dressed to be inconspicuous in the favela, having come from my birthday lunch. It is special for me to be here in Rocinha on my birthday. It reminds me somewhat of another birthday spent in Alice Springs in Australia. Then, my acubra hat was a requirement in the searing sun. Here, the necessity is having police with me for security. In Alice Springs the aborigines were a displaced people and in Rio it seems the people of the favelas have also been left out in the cold. Areas steeped in history and change can be so interesting just like people. I will visit Rocinha another day in more appropriate attire for walking through the surrounds and with more time available.

The Major I am aware, also trained with the FBI in the US and is known to be a very experienced officer in the field. I ask him what is the purpose now of the UPP policing in this favela. He says that it is important they build relations with the community and help to maintain peace here.

People who live here are beginning to get accustomed to the police presence and they are responding positively. The Major knows it will take time because fear was high in the past. Residents did not want to be seen friendly in case of reprisals from the criminals. Nevertheless the difference between Rocinha at its worst and now is noticeable. There are still drug dealers in this area. It is an ongoing process of improvement. The local people will also monitor every action police take here. I speak with other police who patrol the area regularly throughout the day. Some say it can be a difficult assignment but are proud to try and make a difference.

I take some photos with the police who are testing out their English on me, as usual. Some would love to travel abroad. Generally low salaries in Rio make it difficult for people to visit other countries where costs are high. Many are in their late twenties and early thirties, a few are married and with responsibilities towards their young families.

Change is evident - there is a new football area for the community and children can now attend school. The building that once was the home of 'Nem' one of the biggest drug traffickers in Brasil is being altered to house community activities. Another day I will have an opportunity to visit the trafficker's former home. I want to see the local area but, again, I need to have a police escort for this.

Historically, running gun battles were a regular occurrence in these confines as police operations were reputedly discouraged in the 1980s and 1990s. Now the area finally has the chance to be redeveloped under a strong police presence. Plans for sports, running and social events among the whole community and police are planned. In my experience there is nothing like pushing yourself through sport to forget all those social constraints and divides we humans put on ourselves. Uniting through fun is a great way to break down barriers and learn to understand each other. After all if people want to get on and work together there can be no toleration of prejudice.

Antônio Francisco Bonfim Lopes, ake Nem and his gang Amigos dos Amigos (Friends of Friends) were heavily involved in drug trafficking in Rocinha this large sprawling favela. Their territory includes North and West of the city. Amigos dos Amigos were formed in 1998 following the expulsion of a member from the Comando Vermelho (Red Command) gang. He had ordered the murder of another member. Not a good idea as it happens.

Comando Vermelho and Terceiro Comando Puro gangs, working the North and East of the city, are now rivals of Amigos dos Amigos. These are violent criminal groups involved in drugs and arms. On the night BOPE police invaded Rocinha favela Antônio decided not to leave following the initial warnings from BOPE police. Police found Antônio attempting to escape in the trunk of a car. Police said he offered a bribe of 1 million Brasilian rias ($572 US dollars). They declined and 'Nem' was tried and sentenced to 12 years in prison for his involvement in drug trafficking. A lot of drug use and dealing took place in this area before, and now the streets are being made safe again. There will always be someone who wants to replace the leader of such a gang. Status power and money are a big attraction. The continuing pacification of Rocinha may make the price too high for such efforts it is hoped.
I thank the Major who has been very helpful and the other police for their time. I can see they still have much to do but already there are a lot of very obvious and significant changes

here for the better.

One young girl rides her bicycle beside her home close to a stationary police motorbike. This picture depicts how much change has already happened.

The combination would not be seen in the past before the police took over with conviction. The Major invites me back to visit and see what is going on in many of the favelas. I willingly accept his invitation. The history and developments of the favelas fascinate me, as do the people who have resiliently lived and survived here in extreme conditions. The opportunity to see how they can develop is not something I want to miss.

On the way back driving down the winding streets, I ponder over the fact that criminals have such power in such a place as this. One criminal leader in the community determines who may campaign for elections in the favelas or what organisations can work within its confines.

I can imagine it has benefitted some politicians to befriend the drug trafficker such as Nem who could secure a great portion of the 200,000 votes for them! This could have a great bearing on election outcomes and carry a lot of power for criminal gangs, politically.

As we drive along I can hear the now familiar humming sound of motorbikes constantly travelling up and down the streets at speed. This is a new development since the pacification of the favela. Locals have started motorbike taxi businesses to transport people over the narrow steep roughly surfaced streets. I am getting used to Rio driving but not sure I will attempt it myself. It has a unique way of working that I am not yet accustomed to. I'm not scared driving in unusual places and situations at speed but Rio demands 360 degree vision as cars and bikes seem to cross over and back. Despite this, it works and meshed together accompanied by horn blowing it moves forward.

Before reaching the exit from Rocinha I ask my driver to stop after seeing a man with a small boy. I approach him and ask if I can take a photo of him with his son. This would not be possible in the distant past as criminals could react badly to such actions.

The father views my travelling companions with some suspicion. I can see he is checking out who we are and rightly so. People had reasons to be cautious before. I don't look like a local so it possibly helps just now. I am more out of my comfort zone then he is in this situation. The dad watches me as I speak to his son and then agrees to let me photograph the two of them. I tell him in Portuguese just how lovely his son is. That is the truth, he is.

He proudly and lovingly looks at his dark haired boy who is staring wide-eyed and innocent at my camera.

I realise that the fate of this lovely innocent child could now be altered because criminal activity is decreasing in the favela. It is a poignant moment knowing this is what all this work is about - taking care of the innocent and vulnerable. Joining a drug trafficking gang and murdering others can be a thing of the past. He is less at risk of getting involved in criminality and gangs if law and order continues to thrive here. This boy could have a chance to live without the violence that was common before Rocinha pacification at the end of 2011.

He is one of the faces representing the future of the Rocinha favela. There are faces like his in Ireland who need a chance to live without fear of violence and drugs.

Contact

Back home in my apartment it is nice to see a number of messages from family and close friends wishing me well on my birthday. One, who always strikes me as a genuine type of person, has suggested a talk relating to prevention of drug use in their work place.

I like the idea that someone understands and is forward-thinking enough to see the need and possibility of preventing drug misuse and negative consequences. It is a positive communication and adds an air of new possibilities to my evening in Rio. It has got my attention and I will check it out further when I go home. Contact with familiar territory and people is very important to me, even more so when I am away travelling. I value the time taken to send a message to me. It means a lot to know someone is considering how I am. In my travels, I realise more and more that it is people who matter and not material things. As my mother was preparing to leave this life, she remarked, 'remember, you cannot take money with you, there are no pockets in shrouds'. Of course, like most people I like the comforts that money can bring but I understand it is not everything. When I see the poverty and struggles of Rio I understand how fortunate I am to have anyone consider how I am getting on. There are so many who have no one and nothing. They barely have the clothes they stand up in and yet they too find something to smile about when possible.

I look again at the picture of the boy on the beach and realise that we take even simple things like photographs for granted.

Many in poor regions will never be photographed. Many will not even be noticed. Lesson learned - if we are always grateful for what we have, there is always something to be happy about.

8th November - Time Out

I have decided to take time to travel around on my own and speak to local people. I want to get a feel for what it is like to live in Rio de Janeiro as best I can, especially as the favelas and crime are being addressed. It is better to ask, as an outsider to the area, what are the difficulties and benefits of living here in the new Rio. It is easier than I thought to strike up a conversation with people in cafes and along the beach areas that I walk along. Obviously I take the usual risks into account for anyone travelling alone in a different country. I don't know everyone's agenda here but I can get my work done without too much difficulty. Everyone is pleasant and I'm greeted everywhere with a smile that is typical for this city.

It is very busy along the beach areas and this gives me ample opportunity to see how the city dwellers interact with each other and tourists. If you treat them with respect, you'll receive it in return. There are also those with hidden agendas so it is best not to be too complacent.

The beachside cafes and restaurants are busy as always.

When I leave a tip for the waiters it is greeted with a very bright thank you that is humbling at times. I realise that many working at food outlets are paid a low wage and may not have received the chance of a full-time education. Every cent counts to them and they work hard for their money. English is not spoken very much at all but an effort on both parties to communicate gets the business done. I am surprised that although I am visiting their country, residents are somewhat embarrassed or shy if they can't speak English. It is I who should be trying to learn some Portuguese the language spoken here. However I can see that knowing more English could benefit people. It would enable them to open up other possibilities for work especially as Rio is attracting many tourists and visitors at this time.

Having gleaned more information and a clearer view of local life, I head back to my area of Botafogo for a couple more hours visiting my new local haunts.

9th November - Tour/Vidigal, Barra da Tijuca/Jardim Botânico

My now regular travel companions, Elaine from the PMERJ police and my driver set off for Headquarters again. I can catch up on what other work police are involved in generally. There are different operations in progress. Apart from the pacification of the favelas there are the everyday duties you might expect in a thriving city with tourist attractions. Traffic control can impede or help especially major world events and Rio has a great task to perform. General security is important on the streets if people are to visit here.
Rio after all is now attracting investors interested in their oil business and mineral resources not to mention the World Cup and Olympics.

There is time to eat and a coastal fish restaurant is my next stop. Fresh fish is available everywhere. Our driver, who is a keen fisherman, offers welcome advice on the fish as we negotiate the menu. The food is reasonably priced and ample servings are accompanied with extra bread. The standard of toilet facilities vary from place to place, most are fine. In outlying areas, improving services for health and safety will help tourism even further. Here the toilet area is not good by anyone's standards, there is no hand-basin in which to wash hands or paper in the sole outdoor toilet available for males or females eating at the restaurant. It is obviously not maintained adequately. Elaine comments on the lack of adequate hygiene. Nevertheless, we put the thoughts aside and the food is beautifully prepared and cooked. A short walk to the water and I meet a family having fun time together. The beautiful wide-eyed children readily agree to a photo and I've learned most people will welcome the chance of any attention. They smile and giggle as they point to each other's image on the camera.

Having fun at the water does not entail spending money; bathing in picturesque surroundings is enough for most. The mother is busy breastfeeding her new baby while dad takes care of the others. There are five children in total ranging from teens down. They are having so much fun together, swimming and just spending time as a family. IT and electronic games are not so easily acquired by families and that I see as a breath of fresh air.

In Ireland increasing numbers of young people are spending vast amounts of time playing alone on computer games and not enough time with their family. For amusement children here use their brilliant imaginations and also add to their social skills by interacting as a group and with other visitors to the beach. Computer games as we see in Ireland have the potential to become babysitters to children.

In the recovery program where I work sometimes, I see lots of young people with poorer social skills, lonely and unhappy for various reasons. They have a lot of computer games and stay on chat links for hours with their cyber friends.

These young people feel isolated, as their lifestyle doesn't replace the feelings of belonging when people interact with each other.

It is important that time spent together has quality rather than just quantity and doesn't require every new gadget, money or expensive trips, to bring happiness. There are many different family settings where parent's work away from home, are divorced or even deceased.

This does not however, negate poor outcomes for the children. They may be benefiting from the knowledge they are loved and learning skills and behaviours that will bring them through the tough times in life. Low incomes in Brasil and larger families place heavy demands on the parents. This is not unlike Ireland years ago when giving birth to a lot of children was more usual than today's smaller families. People have challenges but how they respond is what makes the difference.

Developing friends outside of the immediate family unit will also add to their overall social skills.

Overprotection and isolation can deprive the children of the opportunity to become more confident in their capabilities to deal with minor and more serious challenges. Where there is financial poverty families learn to overcome the most difficult circumstances as in the favelas. It is astonishing to see and hear what some have lived through. Young people have seen their friends gunned down. Some have had to pull the trigger to have their life spared.

This is a horrendous decision for anyone to have to make, kill your friend or die yourself. There are other young people that were involved in prostitution and whose parents weren't there for them because of drug or alcohol addictions.

Witnessing macroonda or microwaving of rival gang members or innocents who were placed in the centre of tyres and burned to death is not something easily forgotten. Imbibed with substances some enjoyed the horrific spectacle at the time but in their sobriety; relive their part in the horror each day.

Living through the urban warfare on a regular basis has left its own scars and views on life. Fear controlled the movements and actions of the favela inhabitants before pacification nevertheless everyone draws on their inner resources to live as best they can. Not everyone in favelas breaks the law but may work hard to survive. There are many people who grew up in this environment and for them it was the norm, they knew no better so didn't feel wanting. It is funny how our experiences can colour how we view life.

It is nice to see the joy in these young Brasilian faces and the freedom available to them in this place. It is in sharp contrast to the poverty in the favelas and the lack of space and some basic facilities.

I can appreciate how much it means if law and order returns to the favela communities. Watching children grow in a tough environment is difficult for a caring parent.

A little bit further on brings us to a small pier where men are fishing. It may be a national pastime but also it brings food to the home. A young teenager lies resting on the hard concrete. He looks thin and strained, possibly homeless, as I notice much of his belongings are in the shopping trolley. A smiling lady is selling fruit drinks. Her smile reminds me of the man in the moon pictures, wide and friendly. She is anxious that I take her photo only after she opens out her hat fully and brushes down her garments. Her sun-darkened skin is in reverence to how often she is outside selling her soft drinks to the passers-by or people fishing. The lady jokes that if I hang up her photo it will frighten the fish away. A nice sense of humour but it is quite common for people to be a little shy about having their photo taken. An uncertainty prevails that they may not look or dress nice enough. Happy and smiling she waves us goodbye.

Later we travel 50 miles from the city, past a well- known hotel, part of an international chain. This is the city's only beachfront resort located between trendy Barra da Tijuca and the famous Ipanema Beach. The 'Vidigal' favela climbs up the hill to the rear of the hotel. People there have suffered severely from the drug wars and poverty here. As with many of the favelas, Vidigal occupants have one of the most breath-taking views in Rio. The favela faces Ilhas Cagarras and Ipanema Beach, which is popular with tourists. Vidigal climbs across the mountain to connect with Rocinha favela I visited previously.

Further on Grumari hills and mountains surround a beach -

west of Barra da Tijuca and Leblon - It lies within an environmental preservation area.

This area is more expansive and less populated. This is a beautiful beach area approximately 1.5 miles long consisting of white and red sand. It is clean and surrounded by nature and beauty. The presence of big waves here attracts the surfers. Surfing is a major pastime generally in Rio and I've even seen people go out at night in the dark to ride in on the white crested waves but you have to be experienced for that particular nocturnal balancing act.

The water is surprisingly cold so it's a quick walk in bare feet through the icy pools in the hot sun. Barra da Tijuca district will see a lot of visitors as the Olympic competitions are played out here.

On this route we have passed through the residential neighbourhood of Jardim Botânico taking its name from Rio's world famous Botanical Garden. People in this area do not live near a favela, unusual for residents of the city. Many celebrities live here and most residents are seen as upper-middle to upper class. Apartments in this area are expensive by anyone's standards.

Whilst travelling back, there is time to pass through this amazing Botanical garden founded by John VI of Portugal in 1808 and designated as a biosphere reserve by UNESCO in 1992. The 140-hectare park lies at the foot of the Corcovado Mountain on which stands the famous Christ the Redeemer statue. The garden is seen as one of the greatest tropical botanical parks in the world. It is part of the Tijuca National Park. The views from its highest points are breath-taking and Rio stretches out below, surrounded on one side by glistening blue water and a tapestry of buildings on the other. The contrast between poverty, slums and such natural outstanding beauty always catches my attention.

Rio has a complexity of parts from which its people have fought to survive and live. Some do so in abject poverty and a small percentage in opulence. Up to now, it seems this rank system has been accepted as a way of life here - despite the overall cost to Rio's society as a result.

We take the scenic drive back out through the Botanical Garden towards the city. Stopping at a high point awards us another breath-taking view over the water and Rio. Continuing on brings us, again, past favelas where seven have now grown to become one large sprawling mass of slum houses. My driver asks if I want to go through the area and I am keen to see how this region is developing. People are out busy on the streets chatting and going about their business. Life continues on as normal for people living here. There is no sign of the armed militia found in other more violent areas. There is of course criminality but it is less obvious than in some favelas just now.

11th November Sunday – Football

It is very hot today. Lieutenant Yunes is bringing me to see the ladies police team playing football in a nearby town. He is not on duty but has other commitments to take care of soon. My chance to see a sample of Rio's famed football. I'm wearing my official Brasilian football top for the occasion, a bright yellow with a green collar and trim on the short sleeves. BRASIL in large bold green print is written across the front. Brasilians I've found so far prefer to see their country name spelled with an S as in Brasil. A variation with a Z, BRAZIL, is used around the world in English speaking countries. Brasilians do not particularly like this spelling.
'S' it appears is used in the Portuguese language and 'Z' in English.
I will stick with the S after all it is on the front of Brasil's

national football team jersey and that's good enough for me!

Now the fact no one else is wearing a national team jersey to this match has not eluded me but I feel it is time to show my support. After all, Brasil football, what can I say?

Arriving at the indoor football building the Lieutenant introduces me to the team trainer and entrusts me to his care. The trainer is also a captain in the PMERJ police. The lieutenant must leave before the end of the match to be with family and wants to make sure I get home safely. It is a car drive outside of Rio centre. I meet and sit with a girl who teaches English. She is very friendly and tells me she is a bit worried speaking to me in my language for fear she is not good enough. I assure her she is very fluent. Those here who do speak English are uncertain of their command of the language, as they do not have so many opportunities to meet and speak with native English speakers.

The game is tough and involves some falls on a very hard surface. There is no soft landing and the players just get up and play on, even if a little bruised. I am amazed at how they continue on after a heavy fall on the hard floor. There is no clutching of limbs and rolling around in fake agony, as we see in some major European matches or is it that girls don't do that?

The PMERJ police players are strong. You have to be used to playing tough in less glamorous conditions. A player is pushed straight across the railing at the side of the court, landing at my feet.

The barriers are not something you want to run into let alone topple over. This happens to a couple of players, which leaves me to believe that in Europe the playing pitches are somewhat softer for players. The playing hall is more basic than in the city centre. The Celtic Tiger in Ireland saw community and sports halls developed to a high spec. I am enjoying the whole experience of the match here. The heat builds within the walls as the game progresses. They play on, unscathed nevertheless, showing just what level these girls can achieve. I can see why Brasil has become famed for the tenacity and skill of its players. When it's over, the police Captain hails down a taxi to take me back into the centre of Rio. I decide to walk home from there. Walking 10 kilometres gives me more than a slight regret I didn't bring more water as the temperature reaches nearly 40 degrees this day. I find the much needed liquid and some comfort is returned. I'm sure passers-by who glance at my Brasil football top may be forgiven for thinking they missed a great game today. Of course they are correct!

12th November - Rocinha Favela 2nd Visit

My regular PMERJ police travelling companion Elaine and I are returning to Rocinha favela for a closer look. We have settled into a comfortable team and it's always good to meet up. On arrival we explain the purpose of our visit to the UPP police for security reasons. UPP police are permanently stationed at the reclaimed favela entrances. This is one way of monitoring activity and detecting any suspected illegal activities.

The BOPE Police only reclaimed this favela, as recently as The 13th November 2011. It is still in its infancy of change so safety precautions are necessary. I will not visit or indeed be encouraged to go there alone. I promised I would not go there by myself.

I'm streetwise enough to know when taking certain actions are utter stupidity. After all, this is not a game and not a movie. Real people have died and suffered barbarically in the favelas in the past. Like I said before, I do not exactly blend in with blonde hair and pale skin so my visit attracts curiosity sometimes. There are still armed criminals living here in a population of between 100,000 and 200,000 people. Many people get along with their lives but there are others who see quick profit from criminality despite the effects on the community. It happens in every country.

People who live in the favela are curious about visitors. They watch their movements and note any unusual activity. Not all of this inquisitiveness is malevolent. Sometimes children sit at vantage points in the favelas and act as look-outs for the drug gangs. They report police or opposing gang movements. In the favelas still under the criminal regime, there are guidelines for any visitors. On gaining permission to enter, the car window must be fully opened to allow a clear view of all occupants.

Although people enter favelas at their own risk, wealthy visitors who want to buy drugs are welcome but there are also high risks in doing so.

Thankfully we don't need any criminal's permission to enter the newly reclaimed slum.

After driving up the winding street through the shanty buildings, we reach the top of the climb. The major has been called away but a number of very helpful armed police have been assigned to escort me by foot through the streets. I get to see what's at ground level!

Our driver waits for us at the top of the favela. The UPP police lead me down the steep, narrow steps into the heart of the shanty buildings. Three of the UPP police have gone out front and the remaining three follow up behind me with the policewoman. They are very friendly with each other. The police check each corner and empty darkened spaces as we pass by to make sure it's safe to continue. It is a very densely inhabited narrow walk way but we meet no one here.

Initially a number of the police have drawn their weapons. Police here carry weapons in the normal course of their duty but in the favelas they also have heavy-duty weapons. The criminals have been well armed in the past and police cannot take a chance to be unprepared in what is, for them, new territory. As the area falls completely into police control, the normal issue-sized guns replace bigger weapons.

The police are chatty and appear relaxed but they are constantly alert to danger. They can also carry solemn expressions as they carry out their duties.

Running gun battles, shoot-outs and street blockades to ambush police caused major disruption before the beginning of the pacification in the favelas. Innocents have been caught in the crossfire.

PMERJ police now patrol these narrow areas and streets daily and it is their responsibility to retain a good relationship with locals. More and more the representatives of law and order are welcomed. Progress is slow and trust is earned.

Police who were corrupt left a legacy the new UPP units will need to work hard to eliminate.

However the UPP police are determined to make a difference and improve the quality of life for residents. They are taking pride in their work in Rocinha favela and what it has accomplished so far. The recent reclaiming of Rocinha made global news and is documented on TV and the World Wide Web.

Substandard, small shanty houses rise up on either side of us as we make our way down the roughly laid uneven steps. Narrow doors depict the entrances to these small shanty box-shaped dwellings at each level. Electric wiring overhangs loosely from an array of poles. Rubbish runs down gullies from the top of the favela. This is a particular problem when there are heavy rains. The water may gush down the streets due to poor infrastructure. It is a hot day today around 30 degrees. Black bulletproof vests add to the high temperature.

I am perplexed how elderly or those infirm negotiate these streets or steps. It is quite a distance from top to bottom so you become very fit here walking or unfit from staying at home.

Although this is a very populated area we are not meeting many people as we make our way down the steps. I've made sure to wear laced running shoes today for this walk. It is easy to see how a person could fall down the steps or on the streets if not used to how steep and uneven they are Buildings we pass are on top of each other and in no particular order. They remind me of crooked, roughly built dwellings in some of Hansel and Gretel's fairy stories.
Despite this mix there is a different ruggedness about the whole place that holds an attraction for me.

Some people survive with casual work in the better areas of Copacabana and the surrounding beach districts.
Others have, in the past, become involved in criminality. Getting educated has not been a priority where money was scarce to non-existent. The UPP police presence is helping to change how community projects are supported. Children without parents may not be identified before they become runners or look outs for the drug gangs. Just by being here, children can go to school less afraid than before and small businesses can open without fear of extortion.

Visitors and the general public have become interested in the conversion of the favelas. Tours are being arranged to the longest reclaimed favelas such as Santa Teresa, depending on the level of peace and security in these districts.
As the favelas are taken over, other organisations specialising in education, health and social issues are better placed to deal with local needs. The overwhelming effects of criminality on communities have left both physical and

emotional scars. It will take time for trust to build and people to heal. It is understandable that if a person is hurt long enough they find it easier to meet others with suspicion and mistrust. Some will adopt unhealthy behaviours to dull the pain. That is, until they learn another way. It is part of surviving in any home or culture.

Defence walls built by traumatised children can be pulled down through care and support.   Doing what you say you will do consistently with their best intentions   at heart will help build trust. Sensitivity to their needs is required in the process. Without this help, developing relationships will be very difficult, if not impossible.

In Ireland, children have suffered similar childhoods but for some it has been possible with help, to deal with the trauma and move on to live a full and fruitful life.

Here in Rocinha more than any, learning to be suspicious was a skill worth having if you wanted to survive. Empty promises by authorities meant that quite often, residents only received attention from criminals or some crooked politicians, I surmise.

At the height of its lawlessness, Rocinha's alleyways provided cover for shootings and illegal activity. It is a honeycomb of unmapped passageways down winding steep steps that no visitor would negotiate secretly. Shootings between rival gangs and police were a common occurrence in favelas before the UPP police came. I see how impossible it would have been to know where was safe from the guns and bullets. The unbelievable stress people lived under in the past is not easy to quantify. I am once again amazed at the resilience of these people to survive in the most unbearable and fearful circumstances imaginable.

The House That Nem Built

We come to a place better known for previously housing the notorious drug trafficker I mentioned earlier, Antonio Francisco Bonfim Lopes, also known as Nem. As leader of the drug gang in Rio de Janeiro's Rocinha neighbourhood he oversaw a drug empire. He was one of Brasil's most wanted drug traffickers. Prison is where he resides now and his former home has been taken over by the police.

My accompanying UPP police gain access to the building once occupied by 'Nem'.

Its occupants are now all UPP police busy mulling over work papers as we enter.

They are engrossed in their task inside this locked building. The plan is to make use of this space for the community. Walking down steps inside the building, I'm greeted by a nod of heads. After a number of stair flights, I reach the rooftop of the criminal's mansion. I use the word mansion lightly as this is just a larger version of a shantytown home. It is easy to see that despite all the money made from illegal activities, Nem's life experience did not stretch to realising the palatial home he could own. The house shows the signs of having been searched completely by the police following his arrest. It is a basic dwelling but by favela standards is a very big home. A sunken bath or small pool sits in one corner to the left of what was a barbeque fire set in the wall. Luxury at its best in a favela. Nem lived here protected by the other members of his gang Amigo dos Amigos. As leader this was his territory.

I walk to the edge of the roof and wonder how a young man could end up in this position. How much pain and suffering took place in order to provide him with this building.

The rooftop enjoys a view over Rocinha and allows those dwelling within its walls to see from their look-out positions all the surrounding shanty houses. I focus on a green-netted area further on to the right and realise it is a very nicely laid out football playing area covering quite an expanse. Its perimeter is marked in the distance by a high green mesh surrounds. The police explain to me this has been built since Rocinha was taken over by them. It is an area where young people can now play football, sometimes against the UPP police, and enjoy learning new group - not gang - skills. I can see a game is in progress as we speak from this rooftop that once provided a vantage point for drug traffickers with other agendas.

There is an air of positivity at the sight of these young players with one goal in mind, winning their game. Martial arts are as popular and competitions involving police from the UPP units take place regularly. Now there is something better to watch from here.

On the 13th November 2011 this lookout point was not enough however, to prevent Nem from being arrested by the BOPE police. Other criminals were taken into custody thus, opening the way for the pacification of Rocinha. The usual firecrackers to warn of invading police had no impact on the outcome that night as 3,000 police, armoured tanks and helicopters entered the favela.

In my apartment I often see the firecrackers go off in the darkness on the sides of the hills and obviously thought it was some special occasion. Now I know - it is criminals communicating that police operations are underway and they are the targets. Gangs use it also as a way of highlighting opposition gangs are active in their location. Clashes between these groups can lead to brutal conflict resulting in shootings and death as they fight for territorial rights.

I've heard that BOPE police have now started testing drones

over favelas throughout the city of Rio. They are called UAVs in English and in Portuguese VANTS. The VANTS are used to monitor drug trafficking gangs. They will also be tested as a security technique for the upcoming major events such as the World Cup and Olympics and at any other relevant times.

Drones (Vants) are Unmanned Aerial Vehicles (UAVs) and are said to have the capability of flying at 60,000 feet and for a distance of 40,000 square miles per day. It is reported the US used these unarmed drones in Mexico. They are not unlike a spy plane and the positions of criminals can be identified in advance thus reducing the risk of having police unexpectedly fired upon in Rio de Janeiro. Drones are used for reconnaissance and surveillance. The Brasilian Air Force, Brasilian Army and Brasilian Navy first used a unit from 2009 and more have been purchased.
It is suggested surveillance of this type could save lives by avoiding gunfire from drug traffickers and reduce direct unnecessary clashes. Police will be given advance warning of situations that they would not be aware of on foot patrol and so avoid getting shot or killed.

Every favela I visit has one thing in common they are built with some of the best views overlooking Rio. Rocinha is no different.

In some favelas, the shanty homes have been bought and replaced by new homes or hotels to avail of the breath-taking scenery. This has been the case in the West of Rio de Janeiro.

These young police enthusiastically describe their efforts during a normal working day. They are dismayed at a government proposal to disarm them of some of their weapons. Police say not now. Not now, when the criminals are still lurking and dangerous. Not now, when there is still a big risk of being killed by heavily armed gang members. But, maybe in the future, they agree.

We leave saying our farewells to those still working within the former drug house.

We continue on, walking past clothes drying in the warm air hanging from a line outside a house. T- shirts, shorts, stockings and underwear dry along the small pass ways between buildings. There is not too many ways to hide what you have here in such close confines. Houses are perhaps one or two rooms at best, where the whole family live. The walls are uneven and crumbling in some parts, inside and out. The dry weather has made it more feasible to live here. These small structures would not survive so well in other adverse weather conditions.

A young man sitting on a corner stone stands out from the irregular buildings I've been passing by. I ask for his photo. Like I said, it is now more possible to ask such a question. He agrees and politely requests I wait until he puts his light polo top on before I take his photo. It is another moment for me to remember. Even in poverty most people want to retain their dignity, pride and look their best with whatever they have. I naturally wait and when dressed the young man sits as I take it. Lovely dark pools again look back through the lens at me, carrying a smile in this young person. Before the UPP took over, a boy this age would find it more difficult living here with the lure of drugs and criminality. Young boys are known to end up in hardened drug gangs. He asks to see the photo and smiles happily at the results. It is so nice to see him smiling. Such simple pleasures in life that most of us take for granted. Once again being grateful for the smallest things can bring light to an otherwise dismal existence. It is a nice exchange. The UPP police diplomatically wait until I finish, looking pleased. It is nice for them to see how their work is creating possibilities for interaction and a new environment.

We move on to a wider street and I note a number of one-room shops are doing business. The police tell me some have opened since they reclaimed the favela. These are no ordinary shops as we are used in our shopping malls across Europe or in our towns. They are instead a small space generally filled wall to wall with whatever the owner is selling or repairing and open at the front. I pass by such a place where meat hangs down from hooks and the small building walls frame a man as he tends to a customer. It is like a scene from a children's storybook where everything is out of proportion. The man looks very big in this small confined space.

Further along I lean in through another opening where a bespectacled woman sits comfortably in a chair repairing clothes. In this room there are bags of clothes lying around her, filling up whatever free available space there is on the floor or worktops. A young girl lies at her feet on the ground watching television and leans her head back casually to view me. Once again the photo is allowed and the woman smiles as she busily continues sewing.

Another tiny space I pass is crammed with electrical items awaiting repair. A couple of televisions are switched on, blaring out Portuguese onto the street. The entire scene is a bit surreal. It feels strange, as if I am taking photographs of people in a stage performance or one of those purpose built tourist heritage towns except with a twist. I remember visiting one a couple of times outside Port Macquarie in Australia's New South Wales when I worked there. This was a place where people sat in period costume in a makeshift village to relive history to tourists. I feel as if I am recording an important era in the favelas when I take my pictures - a piece of captured history.

Eventually we walk onto bigger streets where Elaine suggests we buy an iced fruit mix. A very enterprising young woman takes our order quietly at her typically small but functioning customer shop. The UPP police decline some refreshment. I watch the childlike anticipation spread across Elaine's face as she waits for her mulberry coloured concoction. I find both the expression and the ice extremely refreshing!

She has obviously tasted this before and her eyes light up, much to my amusement. The fruit is mixed in a blender with other ingredients and put in a plastic cup to be eaten with a small plastic spoon. It tastes delicious and cool on this hot day.

Eating ices - sounds like everyday normality. But not when accompanied by six UPP police who take up vantage points keeping watch while we eat.

We're in between two worlds – the old favela of fear, violence and corruption and the new one of change and opportunity. Further exploration will reveal to which side the balance is shifting.

As if by magic, my driver parks alongside and we are ready to leave after hours walking and chatting through these streets. My police translator is invaluable here, assisting with the more technical interchanges between myself and the UPP police or locals. I say my thanks to these young policemen who have escorted us on our journey and wish them good health in their work. It has been fascinating to see at close hand how the favela is emerging from its dark past. I am impressed at how fast Rocinha has begun its recovery following the initial takeover by the BOPE police. Now the presence of UPP adds a sense of security that can be built on. It is vital UPP police continue to realise how important their role is here, not just to Rocinha but the other favelas and Rio the city.

The operations taking place, if successful, can be replicated not just in Brasil but other countries where acts of wanton violence have become the norm. It is important the UPP police maintain a professional role and continue building relationships with the favela inhabitants in a courteous and caring way. Mutual trust can emerge when behaviour shows people can be trusted. As the old saying goes, 'behaviour never lies'. Ireland has its fair share of trouble too from drugs, alcohol, gangs and lawlessness. It can be changed is the message I take from today's visit to Rocinha.

By evening, I am at my local restaurant, which is a covered outdoor area adjacent to a bigger building. It sits on the corner of my street, a five minute walk from my apartment. Sitting here to my right I see the main routes from the Sugar Loaf Mountain and the beaches of Copacabana, Ipanema and Laguna. In front lies the beautiful area of Botafogo where the run and cycle route trim the water's edge, a yacht bobs up and down in the warm breeze. To the rear the road heads out towards Christ The Redeemer sitting on his mountaintop past Santa Marta favela. He casts a glance across the city, arms spread out in an open gesture encompassing everything before him. I can see the monument from where I sit. It is very visible to Rio's people, poor and rich alike and a reminder of hope. Christianity is alive and well in Brasil and people are not ashamed to quote positive messages from their teachings. Their beliefs have helped them through some very hard times.

To my left are the local stores, cafes and main shopping mall of Botafogo several floors high and well lit up to display what is on sale including many luxury items.
Around the corner a man has made a makeshift bed on legs from pieces of wood. He sleeps there every night on the bare planks, lightly covered by a very thin blanket. Some who are

homeless also congregate around this small square. As night draws in they sit and chat or sleep beside very small kiosks that sell bags, clothes, mobile phone chargers and cakes during daylight hours. These vendor units are built in a row like matchboxes standing on end aligning the small square.

There is no need for coats in Rio as nightfall is still warm. There never is a real winter in Rio de Janeiro, as we know it in Europe. Rain falls some days on different months and the wet season can see deluges of rain and flooding. At these times people living rough will head towards the doorways of buildings or under trees to stay dry. Heavy rains have caused damage in the past as it poured down the hills on the city's outskirts badly damaging some favelas in its wake as mud started to slide. People were hurt and some died as a result.
Generally though, the weather is warm and Rio's summer falls during Europe's winter months.
This time I have the same waiter who doesn't speak English but as usual we achieve our communication goal and I sit back to watch people passing by.
A lady strikes up a conversation with me and she explains she is waiting for her fiancé who, she says, has even better English than her. Turns out she is right! He is fluent in English because of his past work as a guide for wealthy Brasilian tourists in Europe and he is involved in business here in Brasil.

He is a middle-aged man and explains how he met this lady over twenty years before but they drifted apart due to his travelling commitments. Years passed and they led their own lives until they discovered each other again on the Internet.
She is delighted to be back with him and he tells of his amour for her. Listening to their story and about life's challenges that brought them back together, you have to question the existence of fate. It is refreshing to see the open expressions of love between couples or families in Rio. This

couple, like most I have met, are comfortable to speak of love, kindness and even pain. They express their feelings well. He gives me his business card and suggests we all keep in touch.

The exchange puts warmth to my evening, only topped by the food. It is a Brasilian meat dish with vegetables and there is lots of it.

I hear a lot about the preparations in Rio from a business perspective in respect of its economic growth. Big investment is happening in Brasil and in Rio. Some people here also got caught in the world economic difficulties. Now they are planning to bounce back with new business ideas while the spotlight is on Rio.

I hope the wealthy investors who are casting their eyes towards this city remember to include the people of Rio and Brasil in any positive plans. Investment must not be about what they can take from this beautiful area but what difference their money can make to those most in need.

Amazon Rainforest Polluted

The Amazon Rainforest has seen pollution and destruction from companies seeking some of its oil deposits. In 2011 Ecuadorians won a landmark judgment against an oil company ordering it to pay them $18 billion US dollars in compensation punitive damages. The Chevron Company was held accountable for toxic dumping by Texaco its predecessor. The case was originally filed in 1993 and Chevron has still not paid but has taken its assets out of Brasil according to reports.

The Ecuadorians continue to seek that the court's judgment is adhered to. It is amazing how money will blind some to the destruction they are causing. Incredible as they too must live in the same world with the after effects of their handiwork. I ask how can people involved in ravaging some of the most beautiful areas in the world for money converse happily about their so-called 'successes'? The vulgarity of it is astounding. The sound of clinking glasses in expensive hotels does not cover the cries of those affected by any company who misuses their land and environments. I have been disillusioned in the past by the behaviour of such people who take without giving so it remains to be seen who will invest in this new Brasil riding on the crest of a fast rising economy.

1

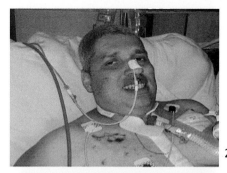

2

3

4

6

5

1. Meeting Lieutenant Yunes on arrival.

2. Friend Alex seriously ill in hospital after double amputation.

3. Young Rio.

4. Botafogo football

5. Botafogo reflects

6. Traffic Police

7. Rio cycling

Rio Traffic

Sugar Loaf Mountain from Botafogo

Mending shoes – always smiling

Lieutenant Yunes

Christ The Redeemer

Carrying water

15

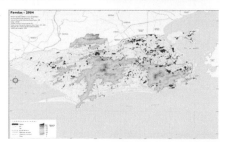

19

20

15. Colonel Pinheiro Neto(former commander of Bope Police, Marie Byrne and Lieutenant Colonel Cândido 16. Microwaving/Macroonda -Death by Burning. 17. Vidigal Favela 18. Favelas Rio (Red) 19. Bope Elite Police Badge 20. Homeless 21. Street Boy

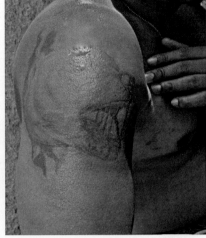

22

23

4

5

26

22.Cockrel's dulled plumes.

23. Reminder of past violence in a favela

24. Director of hospital Colonel Sandinha,
Lieutenant Col. Yunes former director

25. Local animal life

26.Poor and hungry—collect drinks cans

27. Surfing the Waves

27

28

29

30

3

32

33

28.Copacabana - Ipanema warm misty day

29. Selling on the beach

30.Coconut drinks on Copacabana beach

31.Smiles as he brings his beach stalls home .

32. Leblon—water and mountains meet

33.Catching Supper in Leblon.

34.Exercising free on the street.

34

35.Lady selling her wares on the street . 36. Poor and drinking alcohol on the beach . 37. Relax on Copacabara . 38. Beach Volleyball 39. Copacabara—getting fit in the sun. 40. homeless TV watching 41. Dorival Caymimi- 1914-2008 Famous Brasilian singer, musician and painter.

43. Living Life   44. Homeless TV watching
45. UPP police -entrance Rocinha favela
46. UPP police check at Rocinha favela
47. First meeting with Major Santos(former BOPE police) & UPP police in Rocinha favela. My birthday.
48. Constructing new UPP police base in Rocinha favela
49. Rocinha favela homes meet the city

50. Father & Son in Rocinha favela
51. Meeting Rocinha favela locals
52. Family of six - fun by the water
53. Freedom on Rio's waters
54. Graffiti and motorbikes popular in the favel
55. Woman selling drinks on the pier in the sun
56. Fishing in Rio

57. Wealth always close to poverty.
58. Rio view from Botanical Garden.
59. PMERJ police, women's team.
60. Drive home past favela where 7 join together.
61. Christ The Redeemer seen from everywhere in Rio.
62. Favela living.
63. View from the top of Rocinha favela.

*On foot patrol with the UPP in the Rocinha favela.

13th November - Police Academy

My new team-mates arrive on time as always and we head from the city centre out to the Policia Academia, sited close to where Elaine lives. This is the college for police. Lieutenant Yunes has once again arranged my visit without fault. I know this is an added burden on his already busy day but he is trying to accommodate my need to see as much as possible. This way I can form my own opinion about Rio.

They are expecting me, and I am greeted by Captain Lima. He kindly offers us some snacks and yes, 'coffee'. Water can do so much but I like getting the odd cup of coffee. This has caused some humour between me and other police as I daily strive to get in a cup of it between appointments. Sometimes I am unsuccessful as we all head out to our tasks for the day. Of course everyone is very gracious and is doing everything they can to help me. They are all so courteous and excellent hosts.

The Captain is very enthusiastic about the program he is involved with, for police and parents. It has been adapted from the US DARE family program about drugs and alcohol prevention and is translated into Portuguese for their use. I know this program and remember hearing how it is taught, when I trained in the US. The program is now twenty years in use here and the Captain says how important it is that commanders continue to support it. I agree that programs for parents are vital and as Colonel Pinheiro Neto pointed out in an earlier meeting, help is not always readily available when the drug problem takes hold in a family. A familiar situation in Ireland, I believe. This need for help is all the more reason for training adults in early prevention and intervention. The previous favela visit is testament for the need to help parents before the problem deepens.

I have long advocated the power of trained parents working with their own children in order to reduce the possibility of the child developing harmful behaviour. There are some exceptions where parents are misusing drugs and so, need help as much as the child. There are other family behaviours equally hurtful to children that parents may not initially see, or want to see, as having a negative effect on their child. Police may end up dealing with the shortfall for such families. I know from my own work that communities themselves will solve the drug problem, with vital support from the authorities in power. Nevertheless while your waiting do what you can yourself is the motto and entails seeking out what appropriate training is available. Learning about our own behaviour first is vital if we are to understand what we are capable of achieving and what may be holding us back.

These parents must be trained in skills to help them parent in this worldwide current drug culture. Providing this parental and police training helps build community relationships, prevents drug use and reduces the demand for drugs. The overall results are vital. These programs can be used in favelas and give people a way of taking control of their own situations in the home. This kind of training is very important for any adults who work with young people including sports managers, schoolteachers, and youth leaders. Generally anyone who will have responsibility towards a child needs more skills to work effectively in this drug age we all find ourselves in. Learning how to promote the best in a child is a necessity not a luxury. I remember as a Director of Parent to Parent Australia, providing training for police and parents in parenting and drug/alcohol misuse prevention skills. Members of the aboriginal community also took part.

It was possible to see how it worked successfully and in a variety of cultures. Where parents gathered in training groups it was possible for them to learn from each other. Attendees benefited from sharing information and the combined positive energy that evolved at these get-togethers.

I receive very concise information about the program from the Captain who is obviously passionate about providing these workshops. This energy is invaluable and I have seen the results of work by people like him who believe in the benefits and importance of helping parents.

Parents are the biggest influence in a child's life. The Captain wants people to understand how he has seen these programmes help families. He believes it is important to continue having support for the programme. I totally agree with his sentiments.

The Captain presents me with the special arm badge that police wear when involved in drug prevention work. I am deeply honoured and thankful for this gift. These arm badges identify which unit the PMERJ police are members of. They are quite large and encircle the upper arm from the shoulder to the elbow.

There are a variety of police uniforms and colours, all worn with pride, in my experience. All officers at headquarters maintain their uniforms in pristine condition with not a crease to be seen. I am jealous of their ironing talents, which are better than mine. The Captain introduces a group of about twenty PMERJ police singers who sing 'Brasilia' for me as their visitor. They apologise that they did not have much time to practice. I am extremely touched by their efforts to make me feel welcome by displaying some of their extra talents for entertaining.

They are very talented singers and although had no preparation time, are in harmony. It is a pleasure to just sit here and see them perform. The good- natured side of Brasilians once again wins out.

I take leave of this very informed and considerate Captain in order to be driven in an open sided buggy, like a golf cart, to the nearby firing range from where we can hear volleys of shots ringing out. It is now pouring rain and our group spontaneously breaks into laughter at the sight of the young policeman driver who is drying our wet buggy seats by sitting on them first. I think well of his chivalry. A very thoughtful gesture.

Major Robson, whom I met before at HQ, is taking trainee police through their paces on the firing range. The attendees are aged around 20 years upwards. This is a popular age to train as police.

Despite the adverse weather conditions they never slow down. Carrying weapons in all manner of conditions demands skill in handling them safely and effectively. The Major, training the new recruits, tells me he is due to go to Ireland for a particular sporting activity in which he will be taking part. It is a small world.

The general types of weapons used by police are; FAL, rifle originating in Belgium, standard issue, M16A2, rifle, originating in the USA used in special operations, M4 Carbine, originating in the USA, Standard issue. AK47s also have a presence in Brasil.

Taurus Model 605, Revolver, standard issue originating in Brasil. And there is the Taser Pistol that is a non-lethal weapon originating in Brasil and it is standard issue.

There are a variety of other weapons issued regarding riot control, sniper and handguns to units of the military police.

I have seen a report recently that questions the safety of one of the Taurus handguns. It suggests there is a flaw in its make up that in some instances injures the police person in charge of it.

Recently the South African 'Paramount Group' has won the tender to supply Maverick Internal Security Vehicles (ISV) for the State of Rio de Janeiro, to be used by the Special Police Operations Battalion (BOPE) and the Shock Police

Battalion (CHOQUE) within the Military Police, as well as by the Co-ordination of Special Resources (CORE) battalion of the Civil Police. These vehicles have been used in the favela take-overs.

Both the legal and illegal arms trade is substantial for Brasil.

Handguns are normal issue. Police in Brasil are armed in the normal course of their duties but many will never have the need to use their weapon. It is different from Ireland where the general police force (Gardaí) is unarmed. Special units and otherwise trained personnel are the only ones allowed carry firearms in Ireland.

In Brasil private (civilian) possession of fully automatic weapons is prohibited.

Private possession of semi-automatic assault weapons and handguns (pistols and revolvers) is permitted under license to civilians.

My favourite time of the day, lunch, and this time I am joining Lieutenant Colonel Andrea. She has one of the calmest and naturally pleasant dispositions I have ever met. She talks a lot of her sister who is living in Europe.

There is a short time to talk with a police photographer and the officer in charge of mounted police training. There are press personnel to deal with communications and recording events.

Commanding officers have separate eating quarters from regular police and are normally seated either side of a long wooden table. Food here is healthy and includes fewer fats.

Horses are used in crowd control and on other occasions. They play an important role in policing. This equine method will be very relevant when future major events take place. Today some police in the academy are making a presentation on crowd control as part of their examination to elevate to the higher rank of captains.

I am invited to sit with the Lieutenants and hear what the trainee officers have to say on how to maintain safety where there are crowds gathered. Though they are understandably nervous, they begin their twenty minutes presentation.

It includes pictures of police controlling potentially dangerous crowds. They consider further requirements needed for a successful operation.

Large crowds are expected to visit Rio in the coming years especially for the major sporting events. Crowd control is a priority. Big events can give a platform for opportunistic criminals, gangs or ordinary people who want their voices heard. There is a delicate balance between a friendly demonstration and a riot.

The latter can be infiltrated in order to turn a quiet gathering into a vicious and dangerous attack on buildings and people alike.

People can get hurt in the melee, police or civilians. Molotov cocktails, bottles filled with petrol, are sometimes used to cause ultimate damage setting fire to police and at times exploding in the hands of the perpetrator who erupts into a fire ball. Even those approaching police barriers, seemingly innocuously, can be viewed as a threat in an age when kamikaze human bombs are used as the ultimate sacrifice to make a point. Explosives strapped around the waste of the carrier when ignited can blow the head or top part of the body off as it causes a circle of destruction. I remember arriving on the main street in Stockholm late one evening following its first bomb attack.

Sweden has not suffered from wars as other countries. Not all the explosives around the man's waist had gone off so he lay whole but dead on the snow covered ground in this small side lane off the main shopping street. The snow melted from the heat of the explosion around him. Where people are congregating police vigilance is very important in counteracting the damage that could be done by unscrupulous sources.

The examiners today review all efforts and the students are recalled for their performance marks. The Lieutenant Colonel is very positive with her feedback and welcomes my observations.

The young men have put a lot of thought and work into their presentation and it pays off. They are now further along the road to becoming officers. This means a lot to someone in Rio who may also come from a poorer background. It gives the possibility of changing their life for the better.

Being in the police does give some opportunities that are difficult to get otherwise. Training is taken seriously at the Academia where lives will depend on professionalism, knowledge, trusting your work colleagues and appropriate action.

Rio is a very busy city and is developing now more than ever. Lieutenant Col. Andrea expects these men to train professionally in order to command other officers and operations efficiently. The policemen are taking their role seriously and are delighted with their exam results.

I realise from speaking with many in the Rio force that there is often division between lower ranked police and commanding officers. This is not uncommon as one gives the orders and the other must follow.

Sometimes personality dictates the level of working relationships. The officers I know at Head Quarters realise that having a good working environment is crucial.

There are always those who will need to learn how to work better with their comrades. It is the challenge for those in positions of power to ensure this happens. There are continuing steps to improve the police and emanate the new and improved face of the force.

The PMERJ police are organized operationally into Intermediary Commands or Policing Area Command, Military Police Battalions, platoons, companies and administratively in departments.
The battalions are based in major urban centres; companies and platoons are distributed depending on density of city population. The Military Police of Rio de Janeiro is a presence in all of the State's cities.

14th November - Tourist Areas/Policing

Today my visit is to the Police base where Elaine is stationed. Normally she is on duty in some of the tourist areas. Instead she continues to lend necessary support for me to get a true picture. Lieutenant Cândido is in command of this section and there is a lot of respect for him. I've arranged to meet the Lieutenant as they prepare for another holiday weekend in Rio. It is no surprise to hear he is ambassador for the unit. His English is fluent and it is easy therefore to clarify what is the work of the PMERJ police from discussions. As always he is a great host and I get my Brasilian coffee! The Lieutenant explains how his unit covers all the very popular tourist areas we hear about. Places such as Christ the Redeemer on top of Corcovado, the Sugar Loaf Mountain, Copacabana, Ipanema and Leblon beach areas, the airport and many more are included in his brief. These are some of the busiest parts of Rio with a diverse range of needs.
The Sugar Loaf mountaintop is accessed by cable car, requiring safe and orderly queues. The beach areas, where tourists and locals flock, are obvious attractions for others with less honourable intentions. Despite this I have enjoyed all my time in those particular stretches without hindrance.

As poverty is high, tourist areas have offered access to a means for survival. The Lieutenant points out that the actual amount of robberies these days on Copacabana is less than 2 per week, low for the amount of people who visit there. I ask if he believes the reclaiming of the favelas has an influence on this outcome. He believes it has. Criminals in the past came out from the surrounding favelas and areas stealing from locals and unsuspecting visitors.

Knife crime was a regular occurrence in Rio over the years and young people or adults have held people to ransom by knife, demanding their jewellery, money or bags. This is not completely resolved but every effort to tackle crime is having an effect. Lapa I've noticed attracts some of the poor and homeless asking for money from those at local restaurants. A young boy in clothes befitting Oliver Twist, torn and ragged, once asked if I could give him some money for food. His eyes were tired and sunken in his thin body. He pointed repeatedly at his mouth indicating hunger. An elderly lady very worn in appearance did likewise. Homeless people can be found on our own Irish streets too, which is amazing considering Ireland's opulence in recent years in comparison. At the same time revellers are enjoying the delights of the Lapa area, culture, food and entertainment. Everything runs side by side.

In favelas that are run by militiamen and drug traffickers, young people are sent out to sell drugs. An easy way, they believe, to make a lot of money but with expensive consequences for them and the communities.

Rio earned a reputation for violent crime as the poverty and violence became endemic in their burgeoning communities. Children are very vulnerable in these circumstances and all manner of abuse is possible. It is unthinkable that it should continue. Now a seed for peace has been sown and it is growing. The result could allow young people to enjoy childhoods unblemished by fear and violence.

I can see this is a new concept for them and the Lieutenant knows it will take time. I mention how the UPP police I met in the first favela I visited were aware it was important they are careful at all times in how they relate to the community. The Lieutenant is pleased to hear their comments.

He too knows their empathy will play a vital role in the pacification of the areas. It will also make the entire city safer because of reduced crime. The Lieutenant is involved in security for the World Cup and Olympic events as well as his other duties. He must oversee and arrange what happens with his police units. These days there is a substantial police presence throughout the city. I have to say I like to see them patrolling, as I make my way through very populated streets. There are some places where there are less police and local people advise me not to go too far in that particular direction. Another sign they too believe the police presence is making a difference and expansion of this strategy can only improve Rio further. Despite the history of corruption on both sides in the past locals are encouraged by the new freedom afforded by today's actions taking place in their city Rio. Police formerly involved in serious crime with drug traffickers, giving them alibis and weapons will no longer be tolerated according to Colonel Pinheiro Neto and the Lieutenants I've met.

Lieutenant Cândido has served overseas on a UN Mission and is an experienced communicator and diplomatic in his approach. He is an entertaining host but not to be underestimated. The Lieutenant is well educated and has worked his way to this position at a relatively young age for the power he holds. After lunch, which included a very nice Brasilian local dish, I agree to meet again and get some information clarified.

Before leaving I get a chance to see the base where the cameras located on Copacabana and the tourist areas are monitored by PMERJ police. These are seasoned officers who have actively policed these busy streets throughout their careers. Long enough in the job, they take everything in their stride.

Their rugged faces weathered by the sun and long working days steadily watch the screens in front of them. They explain the benefit of having these cameras. These police have the responsibility now of scrutinising activity in these busy areas to detect and prevent any suspected criminal behaviour or assist in apprehending perpetrators.

They can call in re-enforcements quickly where a crime has already occurred. Crime has dropped in Copacabana; nevertheless the role of these cameras is vital to prevention, early intervention and solving of a crime. There are many cameras placed along the waterfront and surrounds. The police show how they zoom in for a closer look when they feel the need. Police on the ground - and there are many - will be best placed to deal with any incident quickly. Cameras have become popular in many countries including Ireland for similar reasons. Rio is using them effectively and helping to lower crime in these densely populated areas.

The Captain, a female this time, from this unit and driver take me back to Botafogo - it is on their way. Another little English lesson as we make our way en route to their Spanish class through the busy traffic. Using the opportunities that can be available as members of the police, such as learning languages gives them more choices in life. They value what they get knowing how hard it can be to do so in other jobs. It is time for another holiday weekend in Rio with a very popular annual Gay Pride parade planned for Copacabana. The police are very satisfied all is in order for the weekend with their units in position to supervise the celebrations quietly but very visibly.

November 15th - 17th - Cycling Time

As before, no point going into the city centre today. I know from experience it will be very quiet and shops are generally closed on a holiday weekend. Instead, I hire out a city bicycle and head out to the well-planned cycle lanes. I still like to keep aware of what is going on around me and remain conscious of where I go when I am on my own. Nevertheless on my travels I am fortunate to meet so many good people, working hard for their income. It is humbling to see people who have so little sometimes, remain good humoured about what they do have. I think of how in Ireland and the rest of Europe we can sometimes dwell too long on what we do not have and miss out on how to enjoy the time we live in. I am not saying it isn't difficult sometimes but the alternative is having a melancholy disposition that is time consuming. A little refocusing would help a lot. Today children are amusing themselves along the waterfront, innocently playing with the drained shells of coconuts.

It has started raining again but I persist with my exercise for the day. It never seems to get cold. My cycle takes me past Leblon. Ipanema and Leblon, sharing the same beach, are two of the most expensive areas in Rio and indeed in Brasil. It is up to 30% more expensive around here in the many restaurants, theatres and shops. Continuing, I reach Lagoa, which means Lagoon in English. It has a cycle lane approximately 7.5 km around the perimeter and is close to Jardim Botânico. It is also another of the few districts that does not have a favela in its affluent surroundings. There are water skiers out on the lakes that are flanked by up-market apartments and rugged mountain scenery.

A young man stands in the water trousers rolled up, fishing with a net - as another is doing exercises nearby off a specially built structure for building strength. Expensive looking gated houses line the street at the end of the water. It is difficult to comprehend the history of crime in Rio when I walk along these streets. The murder, torture, drug trafficking, gunrunning and corruption of the favelas have spilled out onto the same pavements where the wealthy walk. Poverty and suffering are right beside the affluent and those ignorant of the discomforts of their favela neighbours.

Rio has so much to offer with incomparable natural beauty, warm-hearted people and a diverse and rich culture. Their parades are famous the world over. Most of all I am attracted to its mysterious and sometimes open personality. Its people have a right to be able to live safely and be proud of their heritage and environment. Years of misused power have left people in poorer conditions than is in any way acceptable. Now with the world looking on is a good time for people to rectify the damage done in the past.

It has been another warm but very wet day and I've walked many kilometres. I stop off in the metro station where the security officer stands close by while I try to replace my wet outer garments as discreetly as possible.

Rio families spend a lot of time together over this long weekend holiday so organizing anything too official is not a great idea. I can visit some of my new contacts in various pit stops, over the weekend. Despite the shortage of fluent English speakers, it's amazing how much you can communicate with a few words.

After a time, my contacts give me helpful advice and talk openly about life in Rio. I also know I have some other familiar and safe places to go should the need arise.

Apart from business they are generally good company as I take my coffee or shop.

18th November Sunday - Parada Gay de Copacabana

I've been told this is where the big parade is taking place, Copacabana. I've set off walking the 20 minute or so journey from my apartment and meet lots of people heading in the same direction. I arrive to a colourful display of clothes, people, vendors and trucks generally laden with males and transvestites dancing or waving to the crowds. Music blares out over the speakers and adds to the palpable air of excitement.

Large trucks line up on the closed road along the Copacabana beach pavements. Brightly coloured outfits adorn the onlookers. There is a Christian group who are highlighting their views on homosexuality as they calmly walk up the street holding placards aloft. It is a very small group and they are dignified in their protest. The first Pride parade was attended by a handful of people but now it is a very big event. I can see why my contacts in the police say they are used to coping with large crowds.

Everyone is in celebratory mode, laughing and chatting along the thoroughfare. I translate the signage on the trucks that reads Parada Gay de Copacabana and note this is an annual parade. This is the 17th year of (Gay Pride Parade 2012) GLBT Pride in Rio de Janeiro. It attracts an amazing one million visitors including many from overseas. The LGBT community's slogan for this year's parade is "The heart has no prejudice. It has love."

I decide to film the event and photograph the participants, hoping no one will take offence. I'm joking of course as the flamboyant gay crowd love any chance to be in the limelight and happily pose for any number of photographs.
As I film, men on board the passing open-topped trucks start rubbing oil on their shirtless tanned and toned bodies.

Those taking part in this parade have obviously been working out and oil glistens over well-sculpted muscles. I speak with some men attending with their male partners and they comment on the relevance of this parade for them. They want people to accept them and not judge which is what the motto is about this year. There are many who are openly trying to attract potential partners. Some are instantly successful. I hear how it is important for them to look their best at this event and so most of the young males and females are probably in some of the best physical condition of people I have seen in Rio. There is a lot of competition for attention and people have put in a huge effort to be noticed. As I film some who want to remain anonymous cover their faces as they pass.

I take photos of men dressed in figure hugging sequined outfits, some with large wings attached to their back. They pose dramatically for me. Participants in the parade appear to be vying for attention and having an amazing outfit helps achieve their goal. There are transvestites equally beautiful in their attire. It seems the more flamboyant and dramatic the appearance, the better. Not to be outdone, women are out in style. The overall effect of these outfits is spectacular and it is fascinating to mix in with the crowd and feel the atmosphere as popular music is blasted out.

Two men catch my attention, as they stand on the side-line, shirtless. One is wearing a suave looking panama type hat. I speak with them and they are happy to be photographed.
A couple of bystanders also grab my curiosity - especially the tattoos of two smoking pistols and other weapons on his chest and arms. A reminder of the past or a threat of the present, I wonder?
I am also the focus of attention for some who wonder where I'm from with my fair skin and hair. This parade is an

opportunity for the poor to have entertainment at no cost.
They sit on the beach, some drink beer and others play
games with their children. Beautiful brown- eyed children
smile up at the camera. I ask their parent's permission to
photograph them and delighted, they huddle the children
together for the portraits.

Parents are thrilled to be able to show off their children to
anyone who genuinely takes an interest. No matter how
poor, vanity exists as I learn when the mother decides that
her hair looks a mess in one of the photographs. Guess a bad
hair day exists for all women, despite their class, race or
culture.

I feel the connection with this family and their friendliness.
The Gay Pride Parade has been a major event and it passes
without any problems. It gives me a chance to speak openly
with many people and discuss Rio from their perspective.
Strangers but nevertheless connected. As we walk along, the
crowds sing to the music! No fighting, no theft - just singing
and dancing in thousands. It's a moment to relish when you
realise that life can be so good. Over one million people have
attended the parade today.

The other parade even more famous is the Rio Carnival that
attracts two million people to the streets each day.

Samba schools compete with each other on their special day
in the most colourful and beautiful sequined garments, with
even more lavish head ware. Plumes from their costumes
sway as they dance. Lime green, yellows, reds and bright
colours blend to create a rainbow of lush collage moving
along the street. Their drumming band 'bateria' beats out
the rhythm adding to the aesthetics and lyrics for the samba
dancers. Samba is a Brasilian dance that originated in Africa.
It is also popular in the favelas where the western world has
not affected their culture too much.

I've learned police in Rio de Janeiro are used to millions of people on the streets for their own world famous parades. The World Cup and Olympics is just another day at the office.

Parades over and night time is drawing in so time to get back to my local district. At a designated bus stop I board the city bus going to Botafogo and home. Inside the door, beside the driver there is a barrier similar to those turn-styles seen at train stations where you put your ticket in and go through. The ticket I have is not suitable for this bus I discover and it means going to another station to buy one. It's late and I'm not looking forward to walking around looking for ticket sellers at this time. The lady conductor and driver tell me to stay standing outside the barrier in the front of the bus and it moves off. The conductor points to the next station stop but the driver has other plans and allows me to stay on the bus until I get to Botafogo where he drops me off.

It was probably against company rules but he put my safety first. It was human nature at its best.

I thank them profusely for their kindness and set off to catch up with another contact I've made. This unpredictable consideration for my welfare happens repeatedly. There's the elderly lady cooking in a very local café who, although busy, takes the time to give me information about Rio whenever I stop by. She still thinks I am from America, Ireland doesn't register with her. She knows little about it or where it is. It is the small things that matter so much. The vendors who enthusiastically are willing to help with whatever I enquire about make life easier for me. People are at lengths to make sure I understand where I am going when I ask for directions. They will usually add in some advice about where to avoid which is considerate. Even when I just chat with them any one who speaks English will take an inordinate amount of their time to give me as much helpful advice as possible. Surprisingly it doesn't take long to become familiar with those who work along the routes I travel regularly. Despite being a busy city they wave or say hello in Portuguese.

It is putting a large dent in the perception of Rio given by many people before I left for this trip. Rio is not all bad - in fact it's got a lot to offer.

I suppose it's a bit like Ireland in the height of the troubles in Northern Ireland. I remember being in Malta and asked by people how I managed to live in Ireland with all the bombs and shootings every day. It was difficult for them to imagine the main fighting was predominantly confined to a very small piece of the island of Ireland. I lived in the southern part and was thankfully spared witnessing any of the intense violence in the North of Ireland, when I was growing up.

Ireland has seen bloodshed and destruction beyond belief in its day. Rio is not the only city to have atrocities. A lot of people I've met in Rio want to live in peace, safety and be happy. Same wish as the rest of us as I see it.

19th November - Sugar Loaf

I have arranged to meet Lieutenant Cândido at Sugar Loaf Mountain where he is overseeing the police arrangements that morning. I'm taking a taxi for a change - to speed up my travel - but as luck would have it there is a traffic jam going into the small, enclosed parking area of the Sugar Loaf Mountain. It appears busier than usual for some reason. This is a very popular place with tourists and Brasilians. I had hoped to take the cable car to the top but time is passing as I wait impatiently in the traffic jam. I can't find the Lieutenant when I eventually reach my destination! Phone coverage, like in Ireland, can be unreliable in some parts.

In the meantime, I pay attention to activity at the army

facility and naval base in this small arena. Officers in crisp white uniforms are standing to attention in an enclosed area outside their base. After quite some time and a few official comments the Brasilian flag is lowered. On the other end of this car park the army are standing to attention. I don't think I'm imagining it but there are multiples of men and women in a variety of uniforms! I'm unsure what this is in aid of.

I visit the tiny café on the edge of the parking lot where I sit and watch the end of a Brasilian football match. I join in the enthusiastic support with a number of other locals.

It's nice to sit watching one of the most famous football teams in the world, eating local Brasilian food with people in this great city of Rio. I have to remind myself how privileged I am to have managed to get to Brasil and meet these people who come from such interesting backgrounds and heritage.
This is a city also made famous by film director Fernando Meirelles with 'City of God' (Cidade de Deus). This is a Brasilian production made in 2002. For this, Meirelles was nominated for an Academy Award. The film was about the growth of organised crime and drug dealing in the outskirts of Rio. I was given the movie as a present and it gives me another insight of Rio's struggles against criminality.

National Flag Day

All the uniforms explained. It's because today is Flag Day - an important event in Rio when a disused flag is burned at a military facility during a special ceremony on November 19.
The national flag of Brasil (in Portuguese, Bandeira do Brasil) is a blue disc with a starry sky spanned by a curved band. This has an inscription of the national motto inscribed in a yellow rhombus on a green 'field' background.

Brasil officially adopted this design, for its national flag on November 19, 1889. It replaced the flag of the second Empire of Brasil. Each of the flag's stars represents a specific state. There are 27 stars in all. As six new states were added to the country, the flag had to be revised. The new 27-star flag was released in 1992. On the new version, the stars were repositioned slightly. This was to have them displayed in relation to their astrological coordinates.

This is the flag of Brasil that not just the footballers proudly represent in international football, but also others such as Ayrton Senna da Silva and Rubens Barrichello had made famous. Senna has been selected on many occasions as one of the greatest Formula One drivers of all time. Senna was noted for carrying the Brasilian flag at Grand Prix events including his famous win in his home region, São Paulo. He famously won this race despite his gear box being stuck in sixth gear for the final laps. An effort that placed unbelievable physical and mental pressure on him. His iconic presence was an inspiration to the people of Brasil - a bright star to watch despite their personal circumstances. Ayrton Senna was to tragically lose his life, aged just 34, at the San Marino Grand Prix in Italy. He is still celebrated to this day.

Born in 1972 Rubens is one of the world's top Formula One racing drivers and became the world's most experienced driver in Formula One history. This he achieved at the 2008 Turkish Grand Prix. Barichello became the first driver to achieve 300 Grand Prix entries and 300 starts, in 2010. Brasilian athletes have been great ambassadors for their homeland carrying their flag proudly. These men and women prove what can be achieved regardless of where you come from.

Christ The Redeemer

I decide it is better to get a taxi out of here. It's getting quite hectic now anyway. I'm disappointed not to meet the Lieutenant, as this is a good opportunity to see the police operations in place. I hail down a taxi and next stop is 'Christ The Redeemer' on top of Corcovado. It's a sunny day and visibility is perfect this time.

Standing in the queue, I realise it's going to take a couple of hours until I can go in the red train up the mountain. Too long for me to wait so I start asking people for an alternative. In the process I meet a couple from Denmark trying to speed up the visiting process as well. Ulla is a politician in Denmark and she is here as part of a delegation from her country attending a conference called CRIO. Her husband has accompanied her.

We decide, after a few false starts and boarding a wrong bus, to travel together. It seems I was probably meant to meet them, thus the failed meeting with the Lieutenant. I hear now he has kindly waited for me but it couldn't have been helped with the lack of phone coverage earlier at the Sugar Loaf Mountain.

From the beginning I get on well with the Danes. We share transport bringing us further up the mountain where we change to another transport van for the remainder of the journey. Reaching my destination I walk up the remaining steps that lead to the base of this monument synonymous with Rio. I've often wondered what it would be like, what will I see, what is up there and what do people do when they reach the top. 'Christ The Redeemer' is amazing and this time I get the full panoramic view of Rio from the top. It is spectacular and worth the effort to get there. We stand like small ants at the bottom of this gigantic and compelling structure. There is a paved plateau encircling the base and people are milling around looking over the stone balustrades. Far below on any side is the most beautiful scenery that makes up Rio. The layout of buildings, mountains and beaches joining bright blue water is mesmerising. This is another good reason to be in Brasil. I try to take a photograph of my new friends in front of the monument but it necessitates lying on the ground if I want to include the top part, it is so high.

I attempt standing on a low wall to take a better photo but a caretaker quickly asks me to step down. I suggest I could sit on it instead but he good-humouredly wags his finger at me! I give in and go back to taking in the scenery – a worthy pastime.

In the base of 'Christ the Redeemer' there is a door leading into a very small church. It took a lot of imagination to realise this project from the beginning. I'm surprised to hear some building materials came from Sweden. A couple of steps down to the next plateau there is a small shop where commemorative purchases may be made. I buy some presents for home and as usual find pins representing this great place. I collect pins from everywhere I travel to. The quality of the souvenirs is good and tasteful, not tacky. It's possible here to buy some food and drinks at a small restaurant.

There are lots of people and apart from the expected international tourists there are many Brasilians. Police are stationed to provide security for the visitors who come here daily. There is a lovely atmosphere as everyone is in awe of this rightly named 'wonder of the world'. The Danes are equally enthralled as they look at the amazing scenery that stretches out in front of them. The sun is shining and the lovely blue water far below glistens in the sun. It's very beautiful to watch. The Brasilian visitors do not tire of the view either. Christ The Redeemer's arms outstretched in welcome towering above us have the effect of making us feel like children scurrying around a patient parent. There's something comforting about this entire layout.

Ulla and her husband Henrik invite me to dine with them later that evening. It is nice to feel welcome and I willingly agree before they can change their mind.

On the way back they point to a very busy bar and restaurant nearby their hotel on Copacabana. I decide to visit and see what it is like. This is where many of the 'working ladies' or prostitutes tend to gather. It has a busy restaurant with reasonably priced food. Prostitution is legal in Rio and the ladies tend to work on Copacabana where business is brisk because of 'hungry' men staying in the local hotels. Some older local men can afford to wine and dine the girls. The girls see it as business and this is their job. No more, no less. People will do what they can to survive in the midst of crippling poverty. Some will use the money to put themselves through college. Legalising the trade has not made what they have to do to earn money, any more glamorous for them. It is also easier to see that once the women pass a certain age they are quickly overlooked for the younger and more glamorous.

The women realise it's an age-dependent business especially for this busy strip. It's the men that are under illusions that these women actually want them for more than financial reward.

In the toilets I notice one girl is being very sick. She keeps apologising to me for this unsightly vision. I ask if she is ok and she weakly smiles and says she will be. She is tall and spectacularly glamorous looking and has learned to use her looks as a way of making money in prostitution. Though how long she will stay that way, working like this, is hard to say. The girl goes back out to the restaurant.

I notice how she switches on her charm, as a professional,

for the very handsome client as she plays to his ego and desires in exchange for hard cash. The show must go on - despite the dislike of what you are doing, lack of emotional interest and risk to health.

The working girls know that most clients are vain and willing to pay for the illusion that the girls want them for something other than money. They play on this to get more clients. There are lonely men who visit regularly and pay the working girls for their company, someone to talk to. These men may pick the same working girl as often as they can afford to do so.

However I've also heard stories from police where some men had their drinks spiked with drugs and robbed as they used the services of a prostitute in Rio.

Nevertheless I find it sad these young women spend their nights working in this way just for the money and often with revulsion for the clients. They are not immune to infectious illnesses either.

Some of the women chat to me as I sip my coffee with them. They speak about the favelas and new police strategies. They are willing to discuss the business, but photos are not allowed during business hours. I respect their right of privacy. I hear how married men or business people visiting Rio from Europe including Ireland use their services.

I wonder how many bring unwanted problems home to their waiting wives and families. The girls feel the favelas are safer as are the general busy areas in Rio with the pacification in the slums. Interesting to hear they too see a benefit in these police activities. As newer and younger 'working girls' arrive others eye them up and down to check out the competition.

I notice a small girl or boy, I'm unsure which, dressed in three-quarter length coloured shorts, hat with TOMBOY written on it.

A T-shirt with Rio de Janeiro emblazoned on the front finishes off the ensemble, outside the bar restaurant. The bar is open at the front except for a low partition on which the girls usually sit during their breaks or watching for potential customers. There is a happy hour for food between 5pm and 6pm. The working girls can avail of the same free offer as customers. It is good for the restaurant's business attracting males to buy food and drink and a chance to select a girl. I'm curious about the small TOMBOY-hatted person and go outside to ask for a photo.

Though initially bouncing around like a rapper, the person suddenly gets shy when asked.

Despite the language barrier, I communicate a little and give a spontaneous hug before I return to friends.

Janice

The little 'un beckons over a street seller before I get to leave. He has learned to speak English from movies and tells me that the little 'un is a 32 year- old woman named Janice.

He interprets for her that she comes from São Paulo and she has lived in a Rio favela just off Copacabana, for the past 6 months. She is here because there is no room or money for her at home in São Paulo anymore. She has three stars tattooed on her neck, which she says depict her Papa, Mama and doggie.

They are the only relevant things in her life. Her father is now in heaven and her mother stays in São Paulo. Janice has no income and survives by what is given at the restaurant. She tells me she cries every day and is lonely. She knows the girls working the streets and I note they are very caring towards her.

Janice is small for her age, possibly undernourished as a baby and I can see the vulnerability and emotion in her eyes as she talks. Sometimes growth can be stunted by malnourishment due to poverty. The street-vendor translator explains he has a wife and son and they are the only people he trusts. He lives near the airport and must work hard to survive and provide for his family. There are other favelas in that district. It takes a period of time in Rio to acquire the relevant legal status that enables a person work legitimately. This waiting period can be very tough for someone without money to use in the meantime, they say.

The seller knows visitors will come and go but people like Janice and he remain here to seek out a living. Despite everything, Janice wants me to know her heart is in Rio de Janeiro; it is better than São Paulo she tells me. Once again I wished there was more I could do in the face of this poverty.

São Paulo is the largest city in Brasil - and the largest in the Americas and the Southern Hemisphere. According to its population, São Paulo is the world's seventh largest city in the world. The Brasil Grand Prix Formula 1 São Paulo among other major events takes place there. It has been said São Paulo is expected to have the second highest economic growth in the world between 2011 and 2025.

This is looking likely as more and more investors come to Brasil. However, there is extreme poverty in São Paulo too. Heartless criminals run here - a busload of passengers was burned alive this week.

Brasil may be attracting wealthy investors but a lot of money needs reinvesting back into areas that will help solve the social problems.

Young women like Janice and their families could be kept together if more money and care was made available I surmise. It is frustrating to see such need for migration from dire poverty when there is a rising economy. Janice believes the police taking over the favelas made it safer for her to live here. She is testimony to why these projects can and must work.

Time to go 'home' and I take another photo as she sits atop the partition with her sad smile.

This time Janice turns her hat slightly so TOMBOY cannot be seen. Her boyish facade gives her some protection on the streets but now she wants to be seen by me as she really is, a 32 year old female. She gives me a hug and leaves with two working girls. The others tell me they walk her home each night and ensure her safety, when I ask. They tell me not to worry.

The UPP police pacify the favela, where Janice lives. They have a permanent base in the community. If newcomers arrive in the favela it is not unusual for the police to make a house call and check why they are there. It allows them to identify any deviants or unwanted criminals before they set up base. Aside from that new or vulnerable people living alone may need help in the future. It is more possible for her to live in some safety now against a past of violence. She is glad they are there.

Cramped, unsanitary living conditions and no education give poor future prospects, unless they are one of the lucky ones to get famous for their football skills or are educated with a trade.

Once again I'm intrigued how some can make it in life without money or family. I've witnessed people bounce back after the most horrific challenges and pain. Some are actually stronger because of it. Often people are starved of emotional love and support. Parents or peers may want to help but responsibility and love is failed by dependence on drugs or alcohol.

Those who have been robbed of their childhood have to grow up and work out for themselves what a normal healthy relationship is all about. They have to open up and trust all over again. People decide if the risk is worth it or not.

Rio, I can see, has more than its fair share of poverty and the distribution of wealth that appears grossly uneven. As in Ireland, failing to provide proper services for those most in need has only added to their misery. Most could be magically fixed with just political will to do so.

20th November - Cycling

I'm cycling again through the streets of Rio. I don't want to become the latest road kill so I'm carefully managing the process.

The cycling lanes are in the most scenic areas but the rest of the routes need a bit of negotiating in this glorious weather. I'm reminded that the most important things in life do not require money. Focussing on what is good helps make life easier to live and today, most of the good things are free including the weather and views.

Pedalling along I spot the entrance to a favela known as Santa Marta. It has been under the longest control of the UPP police based there for the last four years.

Locals proudly parading t-shirts emblazoned with Santa Marta appear to be promoting their safer home.

There is a lift slowly snaking up the side of the hill to the top of the favela, stopping off at a number of points en route.

The UPP police are on duty at the entrance. I get off my bicycle here and purchase a can of water from a slightly built elderly lady in a small kiosk. She manages to find a cold can in a cooler box and I part with the small fee. Though elderly, she is very alert and friendly. Copacabana is more expensive than where I am now.

My experience is a good one so far and the only difference in more residential areas is people have been even more helpful. Though there is such poverty honesty is common.

The poor are not always 'on the take'. I can see the criminal activity of course. The young or older may feel the need to steal money for food or drugs that have taken them over, neglected children, the violence that remains in some favelas and the assaults against women. Domestic violence is a problem sometimes in areas where other types of violent crime has dissipated. There is the crime against justice when public representatives do not take care. The necessary social support structures needed are not always in place and time ticks on. Like any country it is not everyone who is involved in wrongdoings.

There is a misconception that crime is everywhere here but it is not. It is nice to see so many people who are still proud to be honest rather than proud to have taken advantage of others.

It is surprising to me that in Ireland we have at times given higher accolades to those who misused their positions of power. It is frightening, in my opinion, that we still cow to others cap in hand - begging for reprieve from our debts despite the fact these 'others' were involved in some of their making. These organisations bringing hardship to our nations by running their businesses badly are now benefiting from public money. Yet those who caused the problems give less sympathy to their benefactors in need. There is a lot to be learned from this. Where is our self-worth that we allow this to happen without taking appropriate steps to solve it? What stops us as a nation from asking better for ourselves? In the most unlikely quarters Brasilians, I find respect and honesty.

Brasil has still a strong belief system in Christianity. People try to take its teachings seriously - perhaps that is what is making a difference. I am not advocating any religion, just musing over why I meet people with a sense of trying to do the right thing throughout the city. There is a sense that taking care of your spiritual needs will reflect on how you treat yourself or others – therefore it is encouraged.

I visit my usual pit stop in the city where workers tend to drop in on their way home for snacks or light refreshments. I go here because it allows me to be part of the city's bustle as workers and shoppers finish their daily activities. They descend here to take up position at the few chairs and tables on the wide pavement. The usual girl with the friendliest smile comes to take my order. She speaks no English at all but her warm personality draws people to this small street side café and juice bar. The young men and women serving customers are very helpful and patient, though amused by my efforts to order food in Portuguese. It has become a source of amusement for us all.

Break over and I'm heading back to Copacabana while traffic is quiet. The cycle along the water with a view of the Sugar Loaf Mountain is spectacular as always. Another similarity and one of the nicer ones, Ireland too has its own Sugar Loaf Mountain.

A poor family and a number of homeless people gather under the lone tree, on the banks along the water's edge. It spreads its leafy branches to provide a welcome retreat from the sun. Some are trying to catch fish. The black silhouette of the tree against the bright sky with the dark skinned people busy, around its trunk, reminds me of an oasis.

I cycle to a vendor selling coconuts as drinks to taxi drivers chatting in the shade. I stop briefly, sit on the provided chair beside the men and drink from my green coconut. Waving goodbye I continue on the cycle lane through the streets, past Botafogo football stadium and on to Copacabana I pass lots of people strolling along the street under shade from the heat of the sun.

It's nice to spend the day here and I'm glad now to park my

bicycle.

Danish Delegation

I have a chance to shower and change at a beach side facility before meeting the Danish delegation and my new friends Ulla and Henrik. They are waiting for my arrival, Ulla and her husband have informed the rest of their party of my activities in Rio and are very welcoming. Ulla's husband Henrik is very considerate and well informed on many subjects. There is a feel good factor being here right now. Ulla and Henrik are perceptive around people. The delegation is very curious to know how I find working and travelling around this city where violent crime is said to be rampant.

They ask about my visits to the favelas and if I travel throughout the city on my own. I share with them how helpful the PMERJ police support is when I visit some districts. These are necessary precautions in order to visit places otherwise not recommended especially alone. I assure them I do travel on my own and at night, sometimes by day but I am vigilant as I would anywhere. This is a good time to consider my feelings so far about Rio. I tell them how I love being here amid such a rich culture.

Some of the Danish group lecture in Universities in Denmark. There are a few from the city of Aarhus, which is nominated European City of culture in 2017. The Danish group will be attending the CRIO conference in Rio. This is the ninth edition of the Creativity World Forum and the second edition of the Creativity World Biennale.
According to the information leaflet it says; 'Crio Festival and CRio+ are all about innovation, business and creativity in Rio de Janeiro.

New creative platforms drawing together people from diverse areas, willing to exchange and assimilate knowledge, ideas and experiences and open new perspectives.

Five days of creativity, culture, business, entertainment and innovation. Five days exploring new solutions for the city'.

Ulla hopes Denmark is chosen to host the event following their visit here. She is very enthusiastic about the idea and all the positive international attention that Denmark would attract. I am taken by her enthusiasm for new projects and her energy.

I'm introduced to Klaus Rubin who is very involved in teaching through Drama in a Danish university and elsewhere. Using drama he is able to help people address issues relating to alcohol or substance misuse and the effects on families. Through this technique they can play out their situations and find solutions with support. I'm very interested to hear of his work with the people of Greenland.

Greenland is an autonomous country within the Kingdom of Denmark between the Atlantic Ocean and Arctic. As islands go it is the largest in the world. The Greenland Ice sheet is a vast body covering roughly 80% of the surface of Greenland. Next to the Antarctic Ice sheet it is the second largest sheet in the world.

It is most definitely the opposite weather conditions to Rio de Janeiro.

Despite all the cold, extensive work has taken place there in this sparsely populated and cold and extraordinary environment. Klaus is visiting there after Brasil bringing some amusement at the thought of two extreme temperatures in a short space of time. He wants to see how Rio is counteracting some of its social problems – there maybe something useful to reuse in his own work.

Klaus is an amusing storyteller with a depth of understanding of human nature and he cares. It is refreshing to see someone with real enthusiasm and warmth for what they do. I can identify with the need for leaving aside strategies that do not work and using practical and caring methods to help people. His work is important to improving the welfare of people where he runs his projects. Klaus is using drama to teach math in an innovative way on another project. He promises me I can have the more detailed information on CD. The city of Aarhus has benefited from his creativity where he organised and executed parades and events on its streets and waterway making maximum use of the environment and architecture for the ultimate effect. These cultural and social exchanges bring new ideas and connections that can be built on. With a passion for windsurfing Rio de Janeiro's amazing surfing conditions will capture his attention I tell him.

It is important to understand tourism and visitors are important to Rio – another reason for pacification of the favelas and crime ridden areas. Taking the more tourist route I travel with them by taxi to the settled favela Santa Teresa.

In February 2011 Rio's Governor Sergio Cabral commented, "São Carlos and Santa Teresa can celebrate liberty, they are free from the rule of criminals. Viva Rio!" For this to happen seventeen armoured vehicles, 150 soldiers, 700 military, federal and civil police officers were involved. Their mission was successfully accomplished in one hour. It brings up that question for me again, why were the police not allowed set up this type of operation before? They obviously have the know-how and capability and wanted to do it so what held them back? Political will is a possible answer. Today the quaint yellow bonde, the last streetcar still operating in Rio, travels along the old aqueduct, called the Carioca Aqueduct or Lapa Arches where there are many restaurants and bars.
It passes over cobblestone streets in Santa Teresa, by old mansions, some restored and others derelict. Santa Teresa deteriorated alongside an economic downturn many years

ago and Rio's favelas (slums) spread onto the nearby hillsides. The wealthy people moved to southern neighbourhoods, away from the city centre, to avoid crime. Locals say it is now a very bohemian area with a commanding view over the city. It is popular with tourists and locals and has regained some of its former glory. Santa Teresa has become a popular place to be.

The restaurant blends with its environment, built into the luxurious green and coloured foliage. The view is as expected, stunning. The service is of a high standard and it is a good chance to speak with my new friends. A diverse conversation that covers the relevance of the CRIO conference here to their communities in Denmark ensue the length of this long table. People have travelled from all over the world for tomorrow's conference and are impressed with the positivity that Rio holds towards its culture and heritage.

Walking to the open side of the restaurant I see I am faced towards the twinkling night lights of Rio and on towards Copacabana. Those in the hillside favelas, I can understand, could have difficulty leaving this beauty if their economic conditions and services were improved.

21st November - City Centre

I spend some time shopping in the city centre for souvenirs and other items to bring home. Coffee is a must-buy! It is one of Brasil's biggest exports.

The city is heaving with people and the contrast between poverty and wealth is as obvious as ever. The labyrinth of small closed in market units attracts people in great numbers every day. A few of the stallholders have grown accustomed to seeing me and call out in Portuguese. I don't dally too long at any one point. I know there are a few others in the mix here with slightly less palatable business to attend to. Faces have become familiar as I see the muscled man in vest top and hostile designed tattoos. A thick gold chain hangs around his neck. He is a daily visitor here. Younger men make their way to him every time he arrives, and appear to acknowledge his tough street presence. Police are stationed in the vicinity and I do always find that comforting. All in all I love rambling around watching how people are going about their business. It is rich with all sorts of diversions to amuse me.

Other stores more like the usual European outlets have no sign of recession in Rio. At the Carioca metro station entrance, the homeless sit along walls on the street.
Sometimes the intense heat can emphasise the body odours or urine where hygiene is the least of their problems. There are more men than women in this stretch.

The younger children tend to stay along the road close to the cathedral where tourists visit daily.

Drug Use Rio/Ireland

There are youngsters known to be involved in picking pockets or mugging. Why children so young are in this position is questionable as it always is regardless of which country I'm in - including Ireland. They can range from any age, some as young as eight years of age can live on the street. Projects are trying to deal with these impoverished, neglected children and teenagers. Their dishevelled clothing, undernourished and wan faces watch passers-by. The social system here does not cater adequately for these young ones. If it did perhaps less violent outbursts on the streets and in the favelas would take place. Anger, frustration, hopelessness and drugs combined can be a cocktail for trouble in my experience. I can imagine it played a part in the formation of Rio's reputation for gang violence. I'm introduced to women who work in a shelter in Rio helping the homeless children.

They are busy today, as usual doing what they can to give some hope to those in their care. Basic needs must be catered for such as food, clothing and healthcare. Only then may it be possible to look at their other emotional requirements.

There are children in Ireland who suffer pain and neglect. I've met them as they try to retrieve their futures from the misery of their childhood.

Visit schools in Ireland and see how many children miss a lot of school days, have no food with them or are inadequately dressed for the cold in winter. Others live in homes where there is no retreat from constant negativity, put-downs, taunts, anger and emotional blackmail. There are children who start to misbehave in school, get lower grades or develop behaviours that are unacceptable, a warning sign this child needs help and now. I remember seeing a young boy going to school without breakfast and wearing a short-sleeved t-shirt in minus one degrees temperature.

As Ireland has now one of the highest rates of drug/ alcohol misuse - innocent children suffer neglect as parents lie comatose. Yet adequate funding to help is not always available I've found, to assist them in their efforts to stop using. It has taken those more sensitive to their plight, willing to put in the action and who understand the need to do so who help these people. Charitable fundraising and 'begging' is how some not for profit charities help those afflicted by providing services. This is how the charity I work with has managed to help so many over the years.

I believe that taxes should help provide an adequate social care service and then there would be less need for fundraising. Charities are filling the gaps Government agencies do not cater for. People forget if we don't take care of those addicted we fail to help their children or loved ones when they need us most. There still remains ignorance about what addiction is and who will be the victims. Perhaps it allows people not to deal with it, the greatest denial of all. It is extraordinary that a man has made it to the moon and the worldwide web brings the world into our homes, the good and bad of it. Yet still we appear unable as a race to see the suffering in those who stand or lie before us using what communication skills they have, beseeching us for help. Otherwise we would help more wouldn't we?

The misuse of alcohol or drugs in Ireland, as in Rio, has left families in disarray and desperate circumstances. It affects every aspect of our societies from health, education, law enforcement and social evolution.

Those most vulnerable, the children, take the brunt of the effects of substance abuse on their parents. For some, it is easier to sleep anywhere else than in the same house as their drunken/drugged-up parents. These parents may also be hiding their pain. Other children are not wanted at home or are ignored, as the substances become the main priority. The fear of never knowing what is going to happen leaves their adrenalin running on high. Anxiety and fear becomes their constant bed companion. They are forgotten and left to fend for themselves. Living off their wits is what they know. At a young age they may become the carer. This is the one who cares for the parent under the influence of substances, when the adult is unable to care for themselves - or their offspring. Putting a parent to bed, making sure they eat their dinner or clean them when they are sick are some of the jobs they take on.

Responsibility too soon, a loss of childhood fun and consequences to their emotions - they must learn to deal with growing into adulthood unaided. Other children turn to drugs or alcohol as they struggle to find their worth in a home that impedes their emotional growth and self-esteem. Drug use may not be the problem. Instead it may be an environment of parental initiated put-downs, control, manipulation, and at its worst, sometimes extreme cruelty or torture. Cut to the core, feeling isolated, unlovable, lonely, full of self-doubt, and longing for love, children may turn to drugs or alcohol.

Always the scapegoat for the adult problems where no responsibility is taken - blame on the innocent is easier. Drugs, cutting, self-harm - anything to stop the overwhelming pain they feel. Eventually mirroring their upbringing they may relive old patterns in abusive relationships, unsure of those who genuinely love them.

As they grow they may have difficulty trusting and find relationships confusing. What is a normal healthy relationship, if you have never experienced it? Their parent's dysfunctional example has been the norm and all they know. It will take unravelling to understand what it was all about. How it impacts on their present day decisions will need clarifying. Acting out, getting involved in anti- social behaviour - their sometimes subconscious way of showing how deeply troubled they are. There will be those too who just want to remain unseen in the family background and not 'rock the boat', the people pleaser. Then there will be the children who use substances just because they are available and in their environment.

Young people in these situations are often more vulnerable to exploitation, others are driven to succeed at a cost. I've seen these manifestations in my work with children and adults over the years. Speaking with parents here in Rio I have found they have the same fears for their children, as I am accustomed to hearing worldwide. Overall parents want to do the best job possible and they ask my advice as we chat informally on how they might parent as effectively as possible - especially in today's drug culture.

I have to admire those who are resilient and resourceful enough to get on in life.

As they let go of their fears, trust themselves and choose to participate in healthy, loving relationships they gain emotional freedom. No longer held back by their past. Over analysing people and situations in the hope of avoiding hurt no longer impedes their emotional connection to others. Learning to love ourselves first will lay the foundation for loving others in a healthy way.

"This above all: to thine own self be true, And it must follow, as the night the day, Thou canst not then be false to any man." William Shakespeare.

Now more than ever I appreciate the gracious attitude and gratitude of the homeless boy on the beach with whom I shared lunch. He still found something to smile about and was able to share his feelings with me. I too benefited a lot from this exchange.

A poignant moment that I will remember.

'When we feel love and kindness toward others, it not only makes others feel loved and cared for, but it helps us also to develop inner happiness and peace." - Dali Lama.

Governments need to invest heavily in our most valuable assets – our children and communities. They need this investment in order to even start to scratch the surface of child poverty. For this to happen politicians must step outside the system that cares only for their roles and not the people they represent. Maybe the entrepreneurs investing in Brasil will help. I hear a number of these would like to see a reduction in the negative effects on their city – some may have a social conscience and there are those who dislike how bad it is for business.

There is a lighter side to Rio, shopping.

The streets are thronged at this time on one side of the city centre with well-dressed people who work in the many offices and buildings. A lot of money exchanges hands here. On the other side are the stalls crammed together selling, t-shirts, jewellery and a myriad of gadgets. The centre is a place to be vigilant regarding personal possessions and bags I'm told.

Rio's fashion is geared towards brightly coloured clothes to suit its warmer climate.

Shop-staff greet every client and offer assistance without intrusion or pressure. It comes across more as hospitality than a feeling you are being coerced into buying. I reckon they are grateful people choose their business and let them browse without unwanted attention. I am attending a function tonight so time to shop. After much time in the changing rooms and help from friendly shop assistants, I settle on a new dress and matching high leather sandals, with a subtle hint of gold in them, to make up the ensemble. The dress is a good Brasilian brand in a light terracotta and gold thread. This sleeveless dress finishes just above the knee and tucks neatly into the waist. It is perfect for this evening's cocktail party. The outfit is a good price compared to European rates for a similar standard.

I delay my departure home to Botafogo because the metro has people several lines deep waiting to board for homeward journeys after work. At close of work the transport system feels the pressure. The train arrives on time. I've already experienced rush hour, a bit like London underground at the same time, squeezed in between locals more used to the tight fit, so I pass on it for now. Lieutenant Yunes rings to see what my plans are. It is to hear the familiar voice on the other end of the phone again. It means a lot to have support. I eventually travel home by train and one of my usual doormen is on duty at my well-secured apartment complex. Once inside, I feel completely safe as always and revel in the view of Christ the Redeemer from my room window.

Can't stare out the window all evening though and after a quick change it is revolving doors again to catch tonight's appointment.

Seven minutes by taxi and I arrive to meet my Danish friends. The delegation and I go to one of the more expensive hotels on Ipanema. There is a reception there for conference attendees. As I am covering developments in Rio, I too have been given an invitation. We make our way to the rooftop which has undisturbed views of Ipanema and Copacabana.

We haven't eaten before arrival and so the range of finger food though very tasteful and varied does not suppress our Scandinavian/Irish hunger pangs. We whisper this to our waiter who returns armed with extra supplies!

One of the waiters is fluent in English, which he learned from working on cruise ships. He lost his mother to a heart condition when she was just in her forties. He is not impressed with Rio's health system, especially services for those on low income or poor. He remembers with heartache the struggle to find adequate health care for her when she needed it most.

He is thankful to the tourism trade in Rio for both his job and that of his father who worked as a doorman all his life. He speaks very highly of his father - an obvious role model.

I'm surprised at how open he is to a virtual stranger about his personal details. But that's the same for most here when I show an interest in their lives. There are interesting stories to be told.

Moving into a glass-encircled room with breath- taking views, the ambitious waiter enthusiastically describes his business ideas to me. It involves strategies for tourism and apartment rentals.

Travelling has shown him that less poverty, better health and social systems are possible. He wants to bring a bit of this to Rio and I have no doubt he will! I realise the leftover unused food will be eaten by some of the staff when everyone leaves. Nothing is wasted, thankfully.

22nd November – Crio

Today I'm attending the CRIO conference. I've been given an invitation to attend and will meet my Danish friends there. The taxi driver is somewhat perturbed on receiving the directions. He thinks he knows where the conference is but I have a sinking feeling this will be eventful. Time is running on and traffic in Rio can be slow. The driver waves his arms a lot, speaking loudly in Portuguese the whole way to where he thinks the conference address is. I understand he is telling me that he is confused by what is written down as directions, this goes on and on. On reaching an entrance to the bay area we are now able to ask the security personnel if this is the CRIO conference. They all say yes in Portuguese and with relief I can now leave the driver behind to continue his discussions with himself. In my haste I leave my second pair of sunglasses behind. They are not just a fashion item for me but help protect my eyes that are a bit sensitive to bright sunlight.
The conference registrars ask for some identification to find my name on the list.
They can't find it and to avoid embarrassment decide to let me in.

Inside there is an exhibition of some of Brasil's crafts and cultural effects that are housed in well- built wooden domes.
It is an impressive and colourful presentation of coffees, handmade items, foods and information on Brasil. The Brasilian Government has organised this event and only the best is offered to guests.

These events are becoming more and more important as Brasil and Rio attempt to take their rightful place in the world for culture and heritage - not crime and poverty.

Sometime later I realise I am at the wrong conference, so with some much needed help I get to ascertain where I should be. I'm amused how I have moved past security. Despite the lack of spoken English, I am on the computer in a no-go area trying to locate the correct venue. Maybe the taxi driver had a point! Confusion sorted and taxi trip later I arrive at the CRIO conference just in time to rush in, pay my respects to the Danish delegation, get my security pass, take a look around the displays and organise to meet everyone later in Copacabana.

I am meeting my policewoman translator, at two o clock at the Carioca's metro stop in downtown Rio. Time to leave again.

Arrive at police Headquarters and a meeting with Lieutenant Yunes again. I hear how he must attend an important meeting in his role as Secretary of General Staff in the police. Operations are ongoing in Rio. Meetings take place on a regular basis as planning for the pacification of favelas continues unabated. Police also visit HQ, as matters arising from general policing issues in their regions, needs higher attention. Rio attracts tourists from all over the world and working directly with the tourist industry takes up police time.

Keeping popular areas free from crime is equally important as catering for major world events. If possible depending on work arrangements I will meet with Colonel Pinheiro Neto and finalise some details from my visit here.

I am returning home in a few days so it is important to utilise my remaining days well. I have already changed my flight once and extended my visit. I could consider doing so again but the apartment is needed. It will take a bit of organising to relocate. Nevertheless it is not so difficult to travel to Rio and perhaps there will be another time depending on what life has in store.

We get some lunch in the nearby restaurant. We are a little rushed today as the Lieutenant has a busy schedule and must leave now. There are many meetings and events taking place demanding his attention again. This is after all the Headquarters for all of Rio's police operations – it never sleeps.

Elaine and I decide to visit the beautiful Theatro Municipal (Municipal Theatre). This is an eclectic style building, close to HQ, and was inspired by Paris Opera of Charles Garnier. The names of classic Brasilian artists are inscribed on the outside walls.

Familiar to us all these days, a tax levy was taken in order to build the Theatre following a campaign in 1894. The Theatre did not materialise despite the levy and it was not until the twentieth century that it eventually was built. This beautifully ornate space can now seat 2,361 places and is primarily used for ballet and classical music.

It is magnificent inside and well worth taking time to see the paintings and sculptures in the interior.

The guide brings both of us for a tour of what she describes as one of the finest theatres in the world. She too is trying to perfect her English to increase her opportunities of work. There is so much to see in this theatre, its architecture and cultural representations adorning inside walls commands attention. The performances are well attended and beautifully performed I hear. The Theatre is now home to the Petrobras and Brasilian Symphonic Orchestras. It is a good idea for visitors to see the influences of so many cultures that have left their legacy in Rio and Brasil that makes it a unique and fascinating environment.

We decide it is best to finish for the day and tomorrow I will get to meet Colonel Pinheiro Neto again. My driver weaves his way through heavy traffic to my apartment. The route is lined with busy cars and pedestrians. We pass some nice restaurants and a secure building containing busy office spaces rented by companies and a bank close by. There are well kept apartment blocks and local shops. As always the driver does door-to-door delivery of me and I'm home safe and sound. The journey home takes a very long time in rush hour traffic and going by metro is no less daunting. He puts in a lot of effort on my behalf. I am grateful for his consideration. Normally it is best to wait for traffic to decrease after rush hour but I am meeting my Danish friends in Copacabana in the evening.

Traffic and transport are issues to the fore as Rio prepares for world events. The authorities are aware their present transport system and busy traffic will require their own plan to make movement easier. There is big development due in the city that will cost a lot of money. When it is finished it will replace outdated infrastructure with new. Changes will be made to facilitate growth in this city. This has begun and includes world events that will be staged here. As it is Rio caters for major concerts, parades, conferences and business. Hopefully its throwback to the original explorers and settlers who came here willingly or in slavery will be retained in its rich culture and architecture. It has a unique blend that makes Rio de Janeiro and Brasil very individual.

Evening time, I and my new friends are going to the CRIO conference. There is a social aspect where Brasilian music and finger food are aplenty. The music is a bit deafening. Most people go outside having a desire to talk or eat in the warm air. Having reviewed the cultural entertainment, we realise our appetites are again too big for small portions – no insult to the organisers. It's time to leave in search of more substantial food.

Arriving in Lapa again there is a number of bars/ restaurants with public samba and salsa dancing. Visiting local establishments, shops and restaurants is the best way to see the real Rio's entertainment. Locals here are amazed to hear their dances especially Salsa are now the trend in Europe. It is not an easy task to dance like them.These Brasilians are experienced and take their moves seriously as they glide sensuously across the floor regardless of body shape or height. This is a challenge for inexperienced Europeans despite being light of foot.

It may start out smooth but can slide easily into wrangling for balance with your dancing partner if you are not focused. Smiling in this position is an even bigger test on the inexperienced. Locals like to see visitors try out their dance routines and think it complimentary of their cultural activities. How right they are! The funny side is not lost on them either.

The restaurant food portions are so large here it is easier to share our orders. Serving waiters tend to be men - the main breadwinners in most families. As usual they cannot be helpful enough. Naturally perceptive they are quick to note how best to serve their customers. They are grateful too for the tips that boost their meager wages.

After dinner some friendly girls celebrating their birthday share the celebration cake with us. More discussions about Rio continue.

A walk is necessary to knock off some of the extra kilos we all just acquired. There are two girls, one dressed as Michael Jackson and the other as a monster, performing to the soundtrack of 'Thriller'. It's late for two young girls to be out on the streets I think. This busking is outside a busy restaurant to attract the attention and donations of the clientele.

One of the Danish delegation, Klaus, with his artistic observational skills, commented on the stooped roughly clad man passing the performance. He notes how difficult it is at times in this complex city of poverty and wealth, to tell theatre from reality. I follow his gaze and sure enough, the old man could well have been part of the theatre performance on the street. Reality is sometimes stranger in Rio. Life here is shaped by its past and now its future. Easy to believe it is all one big stage production that includes a vast range of activities all running at the same time. My friends too love how this city meshes together its rich culture, warmth, old architecture and vibrant will to live. In all that it faces, good and bad, Rio de Janeiro is very much alive. Time for our taxi home, an early start in the morning again. Lieutenant Yunes contacts me to discuss my arrangements for morning. As always the Lieutenant is well organised. I will visit Santa Marta favela, situated close to where I live, and have a chance to see how it is four years on, following reclamation by BOPE police and pacification by UPP police.

23rd November - Santa Marta Favela

Up bright and early as usual here, I am ready on time. It's the chance of new adventures and so much to see that motivates me once again.
Elaine is on time as always. We drive to the entrance of the Santa Marta favela and begin the steep drive up to the top. There is a lift for local people and visitors. It works its way up tracks on the side of the hill, with some drop off points. This lift makes a great difference to those living in the favela

as well as visitors.

Nearing the top, we stop the car to take in the beautiful scenery in front of us. The Sugar Loaf Mountain lies below in picturesque surroundings. Blue water glints in the bright sunlight. I can see how developers would like to own these mountain areas. The favelas are on prime locations around Rio. People would pay a lot in order to inhabit any such redeveloped areas. There have been rumours that developers have tried to acquire lands such as these. Building here would have great prospects. So far the police I met continue reclaiming the favelas and maintain them as they are for their residents.

There are regions where people have sold their small piece of land for business development.

In Ireland we saw the corruption associated with planning and construction in some cases. Where money is concerned there is always someone with a hidden agenda. Nevertheless these residents continue to live here and Santa Marta favela is beginning to thrive. It is now held up as one of the reclamation success stories.

Ten Gabriele welcomes me at the UPP police base in Santa Marta. He is escorting us down through the favela today. We gather our rations of water for the walk. This is crucial because of the high temperatures. Humidity in the favelas makes it even more uncomfortable to walk in such cramped surroundings.

There is no air conditioning here in these small shanty houses. Air circulates through the small glassless curtained windows. I take a slight detour into an even narrower lane between buildings. An unusually big rat is rooting around ignoring my presence.

Lack of proper sanitation, basic water and toilet facilities attract vermin. Some rubbish is carried by water down the adapted water gullies to the bottom of the favela. Regardless, there appears to be no stench despite the humidity. These human issues have come to light as the criminality decreased here. Work for a living or crime? There is always an element of choice available.

A well-built local man in orange-coloured overalls is sweeping up any litter along the path. He agrees to be photographed. I wonder why he doesn't smile as I press the button. As I finish a wide grin spreads across his face. I see he is missing a number of front teeth.

I understand now he is uncomfortable to let his lack of molars be recorded. Like us all he wants to look well. Ten Gabriele explains how local people are involved in practical projects to improve their living conditions through education. He points out newly painted buildings that are bright and cheery in the sunshine. The buildings do not carry the depressing look of other favelas yet to be pacified.

There is a feeling of freedom in this one. It is obvious police officers efforts has resulted in good relations with favela's residents. Greetings towards them are friendly and that must be a big relief for everyone including me at this moment. Ten Gabriele sees his role is to continue building on their successes with locals if vital integration is to happen. He genuinely cares that this is achieved. It is part of his mission here he says. The friendliness from locals is not feigned. I feel the UPP police are well selected overall for their role.

United co-operation makes Santa Marta a success story. These are the opening chapters and are already best sellers!

From the top of the favela I can see an all-weather green coloured football pitch where a few young boys are playing. This pitch is enclosed by green mesh, and an adult is giving them some football tips on the marked-out playing surface. I can see the boys are enjoying learning new skills - having fun with their friends without any threat. I mention how clean and well laid out this area is. It is unlike other un-pacified favelas. Before pacification here, crime was rampant.

Gang wars were so brutal that I'm told how a clash of gangs led to the murder and decapitation of a member. Opposition criminals used his head to play football on the same pitch - happily the area is now being used by youths for healthy sports as I stand and watch. They support a Rio football team in the top division they say.

A better occupation for young people, I'm sure! The brutal death was not an isolated incident. It is with determination such unfeeling torture has been eliminated in this favela. I wonder how the parents of those killed learn to live with such barbaric cruelty. A major achievement has taken place here in just four years. Thankfully police now only need to carry their standard issue Taurus pistols as peace continues to build. I can hear singing coming from a big building. People of varying ages congregate to practice for an event in the favela.

Since the area calmed, there are many courses and social activities available to residents. It is hoped they will be able to access education and social supports more easily. We meet visitors from Israel, who have travelled here to see how the favelas are developing without crime. Two local people are acting as guides for them. This is a new initiative to bring tourists to the area, controlled by the residents. All the local guides wear t-shirts with the group's name printed on them. We stop and talk for a while. The visitors mention how remarkable it is to see this area in a new light. They see the possibilities when resources are employed for better use such as this.

I stop at a small stand where a mix of trivial items is being sold. I buy some small keepsakes to give something back to this community.

There is the feeling that a community spirit of togetherness is building. Smiling children in particular like the playful attention the police give them.

A man is bathing his child in the tiny space outside the door of his home. Water is not on tap here so he washes in the tin bath outside in the afternoon sun. This is not unlike Ireland in the past when tap water and money was in scarce supply too.

In time of recession we may have to learn some old skills perhaps.

Bright coloured clothes washed and clean hang from short clothes lines at varying angles between the shanty houses.

Two women are chatting on the steps. One carries her carrier bag over her handless arm. I notice both her hands have been removed at the wrist. I wonder how she manages even the simplest chore. Life has been very hard for some.

It is a steep walk down the steps to the next level where the pride and joy of this community stands aloft. It is a statue of Michael Jackson and a mural of him adorns the adjacent wall with 'Neverland' printed on it. Both are fiercely maintained against vandalism and graffiti.

Santa Marta was one of two locations where Michael Jackson recorded the controversial song: 'They don't care about us.' Jackson was strongly accused in the US of including anti-Semitic lyrics and was forced to apologise. He later rerecorded the song with some alterations. Residents were happy to have Jackson record in their favela and saw it as a way of having their situation highlighted publicly. Where his statue stands is another great vantage point to view the city of Rio below.

Further on, a less than friendly looking teenager watches us from his doorstep. It is possible to see a glimmer of how threatening it must have been at its height. I decide to talk with him. I comment he is wearing new football boots. His demeanour suddenly softens as he talks about his favourite subject - football.

He doesn't speak English but knows how to communicate fervour for his favourite team. Police officer Ten Gabriel translates the more difficult parts of the conversation.

There is always something that levels the ground for us. Football and fun – it is a way of communicating to all age groups. Here, it helps build trust as police take on local teams in football matches.

There is a lot of work in progress from construction to cleaning. The buildings are receiving coats of bright paint: Yellows, reds, blues and other eye-catching shades. It is changing the face of the buildings - a kaleidoscope of colour to replace the old grey shanty look.

Haas & Hahn is the working title of artistic duo Jeroen Koolhaas and Dre Urhahn from the Netherlands. They brought this work to the favela. So much can change because of one person or in this case, two. It is difficult to remember the torture and death that took place here when you see all the brightly coloured buildings. It's a new day and a new way in Santa Marta.

I recall one of my favourite walks in Stockholm, along the river Årsta Viken. In its former life it was an industrial area on the water that attracted anti-social behaviour. A clever decision allowed the construction of small wooden summer homes overlooking the water and in the park. To live here in the summer entails planting flowers around the mini wooden summer homes. It became a most colourful refuge from city life. Once inhabited and flowers bloomed, the anti-social behaviour disappeared.

It is now one of the most treasured areas of Stockholm - on the island of Södermalm beside where I lived, when time allowed. Changing the face of misery and abandonment with brightness, as in Stockholm and now Santa Marta, attracts positive attention. Ideas for improving their economic circumstances are being generated by these changes. There is an old saying, 'Fake it till you make it'.

Santa Marta like my walk beside Årsta Viken has recreated itself into an inviting and less fearful place to visit. Most definitely the police intervention here has played a pivotal role in this achievement. Local people are now building and creating a new more welcoming and safer environment to live in or visit.

I see a street name, the first I've come across, Rua Meaning Street, 'do côco verde' (green coconut). It means 'the street of the green coconut' in translation. In translation it means, 'The street of the green coconut'.

Coconuts are very common in Rio; street vendors sell them. The coconuts can be cut with a machete in front of customers as required. This ensures freshness. A straw is then inserted for customers to drink the refreshing and cheap coconut water.

Coconut water has high potassium content. Some of the other ingredients that are biologically active in coconut water include L-arginine, ascorbic acid and magnesium. L-arginine is a substance that gyms are familiar with. Here it is used in its natural form - part of the green coconut. The coconut is a source of food - a feature all along streets in Rio especially around beaches.

It's so popular and common in Rio that it seems fitting that the residents named the favela street after it.

It is becoming more and more important for the favelas to have an identity of their own. Street names are now important in that process.

In favelas such as Rocinha and Santa Marta, post was not delivered to each door, a mind-blowing task to say the least. Apart from the lack of street names and addresses to find postal recipients, it would take a brave postal worker to wander around crime-infested favelas.

Post was generally left at one building on the bottom level and people collected it there. Now as these areas settle the wish for street names is arising. It is still complex to find where they are, but people want their street recognised. It's a big change from the past dark secrets and hidden alcoves.

I sip the necessary water walking back up the steep steps. I'm grateful for the relief it affords as the cool drink moistens my parched throat in this heat. I spot a slim man taking a break from painting. The poorer people in Rio can sometimes look the fittest - a basic diet, manual labour and climbing up and down these steps daily is a sure way of staying trim.

The man sits languishing against the wall smoking a cigarette, legs stretched out before him in his baggy orange pants. Spirals of smoke slowly rise in the warm air. I tell him he reminds me of Michael Jackson because of his dark, curly hair. He understands and his two companions, who are listening closely, repeat the name over and over through peals of laughter. He is not in the least offended, perhaps a little shy, with his new found fame. He allows me take his photograph. I am careful to ask permission when taking photographs of people as usual. I need to keep in mind their right to privacy and don't wish to be offensive or create a situation. Since Santa Marta has been pacified, it has attracted huge interest from overseas visitors intrigued by favela history.

Before entering you are advised not to take photographs. There are people living here still sensitive to any publicity because of their past. Locals are careful in case of exploitation. They have seen their fair share of it. I am fortunate everyone so far has decided to respond enthusiastically to my intrusions into their world. It is really nice of them to trust I will use the results carefully.

Not all the favelas are pacified. In these unpacified favelas it is necessary to be aware that urban warfare is played out daily. They are not playing games nor are they interested in being photographed.

Photographs and reporting criminality was enough to see Tim Lopes murdered by drug gangs. There are very criminally active favelas still under the control of gangs where weapons and drugs are their business.

Further up the steps a lady is hanging out her washing. She is wearing Minnie Mouse ears. She looks happy and natural going about her chores. There is an almost Disney-like atmosphere to this once tortured place.

As we climb I can hear loud music coming from a small home. Considering all the homes are built in close proximity it is amazing to hear it's quite a few decibels higher than I'd expect. The sound carries across the favela. A woman framed by her green, glassless window, keeps a watchful eye on her two children. Her small cerise pink curtain adds bright colour draped against her dark skinned face. She shyly says she loves music and it appears the neighbours must too. Her children dance around in front of me eager to be photographed, with her consent. The children look so happy in their neon clothes with braided hair and mischievous smiles. None of the pressures of urban warfare show on their young faces. The chance instead of a better future now looks clearer. This moment I feel must be remembered. Natural happiness and open childlike expressions dance across their young faces.

I make it back to the UPP police base at the top of the favela where the visiting Israelis await. Ten Gabriele takes the time to show us footage of the work before and after their arrival in Santa Marta. Of course the police are anxious for people to see their progress here.

Ten Gabriele does a very good presentation showing video footage of the BOPE police taking back the favelas. It shows the face of urban warfare, arrests and the eventual pacification by the UPP.

Even attracting the European artists to use their skills of paint and colour in the favela is an achievement in itself. Visually Santa Marta looks and is cleaner because locals have a newfound pride in their locality. There are still some problems, no one is denying that. Overall it is different and for the better. Visiting here is giving me a perception of what is possible in the most difficult circumstances. There is much to take away from this to be used in my own work.
Time is moving on but we still meet again with Lieutenant Yunes at HQ. He, like his fellow officers has a burgeoning schedule. A lot of decisions to be made here plus the usual mountain of paperwork and reports. He doesn't waste time.

Sugar Loaf Mountain

The afternoon is free to visit the famous Rio landmark, Sugar Loaf Mountain. I can't tell if Elaine or I is more excited about it. She has been here before but is still as appreciative of its beauty as when first she saw it! Like landmarks in most countries - the closer we are, the less we go there until visitors arrive.
Elaine's enthusiasm is infectious and adds to the whole experience. Though my business in Rio is serious I always find time to relax and laugh with my new contacts. These new friendships and old I will take home from Rio.

The queue is not long at this time and soon we are in the windowed cable car shunting up on the first leg of the ascent. It is on our final stop on the top of the Sugar Loaf that the full beauty of Rio, in panorama, is evident. The view is spectacular. Our altitude is such that misted-topped mountains appear small at the bottom.

Christ The Redeemer on Corcovado looks tiny from here and boats are just small specs in the clear blue water below. Cooler air circulates around us and we lean against the railing to take in the spectacle. I want to remember standing here, the nice memories of Rio and how special it is.

There is seating at the top and people relax in the stunning surroundings, with friends or family. There is a small café and an information centre.

It has the history of the cable cars and scenic mountaintop on display. Sugar Loaf Mountain attracts visitors from all over the world and is a lucrative development, using natural resources and imaginative thinkers. On one side soldiers parade far below. The other direction sees boats bob up and down where Copacabana and Ipanema's pale sands form a border between land and sea.

The favelas, hotels and apartments huddle together, nestled against the mountains with a light cloak of mist giving a surreal look to the picture.

I recall the movie 'Gorillas In The Mist' with a similar view of mountaintops covered in soft white veils of mist.

It must have been an awesome sight that greeted those explorers who landed here. All those years ago did they realise how Rio would develop. They were visionaries willing to enter the unknown for adventure and wealth.

It is time to go to the police base at Copacabana. We hop back on the cable cars and take in the view as we slowly descend.

Lieutenant Cândido is accompanying me to HQ for my final visit there. I tell the Lieutenant of my observations, views and meetings in Rio. He remarks on my frequent use of the work 'impressive'.

I AM genuinely impressed and that doesn't happen easily for me these days. I have seen a lot on my travels over the years that did not stand up to what it said on paper. I have met with and spoken to so many people who believe that life in Rio has improved, mainly because of the operations of the police in the favelas. It is extraordinary but locals mention police protection and more peaceful patrolling as the main reason for the change in crime. There are still complaints about excess force nevertheless anyone I talked to want the police to continue helping.

Rio is safer and better since the BOPE Police first started their forays into the drug gang's territory and began to reclaim it. The UPP's follow-up projects building relationships maintain a sense of calm. This continues the positive progression in the favelas I feel. At last, people can begin to live without fear. Working together and learning to trust is the challenge but will undoubtedly help. Learning to trust again after being hurt is a human condition. A heavy weight lies on police shoulders to make these missions work. It is now time for those in power to add their lot to the pot and make this sustainable. Hopefully the world media will continue to follow the safeguarding of Rio long after the big events pass. People matter here. This is important.

Money is needed from Brasil's and Rio's governing parties to provide adequate wages, healthcare, social welfare support, policing, education and new opportunities. I live in hope they will do the right thing!

We arrive at HQ and Elaine and I say our tearful goodbyes. She must catch her bus home. Her friendship, humour and personality will make me miss her enormously. I will meet her again someday, I tell her. Dabbing her eyes she sets off for home.

However, I see Elaine sooner than I expect as she became the target of a robbery. She runs back to HQ to tell the Lieutenant that her handbag has been stolen at knifepoint by two youths as she walked to her bus. Such a coincidence this happens now.

Immediately, a police car is dispatched carrying Elaine, it returns 15 minutes later with her bag and all its contents. She managed to identify them.

Be it for drugs or food turning to crime can seem like the easier solution. Decreasing these social problems will in my experience and from what I have witnessed in the city, reduce crime even further.

I am relieved that her bag has been recovered but a little worried about her. She is naturally upset but glad she got her bag back. I'm confident she will be ok but any robbery puts a dent in your faith in humans, for a while anyway. It is an invasion into a person's private life that in turn affects how safe we feel.

HQ/Officers Final Meeting

Now time to meet Lieutenant Colonel Yunes and Colonel Pinheiro Neto who is here today.

I meet familiar faces in HQ as we wait in the Lieutenant's office. There is business to complete before home time for the officers.

On this last meeting Lieutenant Colonel Cândido, Lieutenant Colonel Yunes, Lieutenant Colonel Junior and Colonel Pinheiro Neto are present.

I cannot suppress a smile meeting Colonel Pinheiro Neto. I have respect for what he and others are trying to achieve here. We greet each other warmly and it is another pleasant meeting. He is interested to hear my honest findings of Rio and expects I will not dress it up for his sake. The truth is expected.

I can work with that anytime. Avoidance and continuous lies doesn't inspire me. They're like a cold shower.

I tell the story of the young man on the beach, Janice from São Paulo and numerous others who spoke of the benefits of the pacified favelas. I candidly tell them how some have spoken of corruption in police but none had personal experiences of this. Documented police incidents have occurred but overall everyone I met regardless of socio economic divide prefer having their protection. These people believe it makes life easier wherever they are based. From the poorest to the wealthiest they feel Rio has become safer. There is still a lot of work to be done but this is the beginning of substantial change for the city. People want to see this political interest in their well-being.

All locals spoken to could see and openly describe the initiatives are decreasing crime both in the favelas and in the surrounding areas. That is some achievement in such short time.
These police are pleased with the feedback, as they don't often hear the positive comments from the streets they patrol. Nothing new in that situation I realise. Hearing it from a third party lends a note of honest local appreciation for their interventions. It is not fabricated for anyone's benefit.

There is a value in that, there has to be. Police have lost their lives here in the line of duty. Families were left without a father or mother. Recognition for what is done right is always a strong encouragement to repeat more of it. None of the people I spoke to and questioned closely in Rio, were aware of my connections with the police here, I these officers. All remarks give a true and positive appraisal of the situation.

Once again I use the word 'Impressed' and I am. Having seen drug problems spiral out of control in Ireland giving it one of the highest rates in Europe, I am impressed at what can be achieved with the right people and sufficient resources.

I have been around politics in various countries long enough to know that often those on the ground are forgotten by governments in their ivory towers.

I acknowledge there is a lot to be done here in Rio. This problem has emerged over many years through poverty, neglect and corruption. I have seen a lot of drug problems and criminality over the years working in this field. I see it in Ireland and in other countries. The unseen criminality is often by those who could start change but won't, who could invest in helping, but do not. I view this as the biggest crime of all.

The police task of safeguarding Rio is an onerous and long-term mission but will show just rewards in the end.

There is still serious crime and it is being addressed according to available resources.

It takes time for people to realise the need to change their attitudes. It will help when they learn it is necessary to let go of the old ways and work together and make Rio a safer place. The process has begun.

Visitors still need to be cautious when travelling but in saying that, the same applies to most countries worldwide.

I give my friends small gifts that they open straight away. One of these is a t-shirt with the four seasons of Ireland on the front, depicting sheep holding an umbrella to ward off the rain. Each season looks similar. I ask the Colonel, former head of BOPE police - one of the toughest units in the world

- if he'll wear it. His eyes show merriment as he somberly declares in an authoritative tone that he will - but under his uniform.

At the outset I told them I wanted to take a couple of photos and write an article for a newspaper. As I travelled around I realised it would be an injustice to Rio, the police, communities and what is actually happening here were I to limit it to that. It has become personal to me. How Rio de Janeiro is supported for the sake of its people is relevant not just to them but the rest of the world.

I want successful outcomes for these warm, hardworking and resilient people with their human vulnerabilities. I've looked into many eyes in Rio as they speak of their hardships, needs and will to make opportunities happen.

The possibility of extreme violence is not in Rio it is in humans - worldwide certain conditions allow the growth and justification of surviving at the expense of another's pain. It doesn't have to be this way. There is a choice. Power is not achieved by putting down or hurting others, that is fear, cowardice and weakness – it is instead by learning to take care towards others and ourselves as we travel on our chosen paths. There is power when we develop the strength to overcome traumas and pain and most of all to learn from them.

Courage is needed to face our fears in order to understand that we will survive and grow. Spirituality, not necessarily organised religions, plays a part for those who seek guidelines on living.

The Dalai Lama, when asked what surprised him most about humanity answered, "*Man. Because he sacrifices his health in order to make money. Then he sacrifices money to recuperate his health. And then he is so anxious about the future that he does not live in the present or the future; he lives as if he is never going to die, and then dies having never really lived.*"

These men, officers, view some photos I have taken of people now living in the reclaimed favelas. They check them carefully to see what they portray. I show the young child in his father's arms as he looks lovingly at his son in Rocinha favela. This I see represents what it must be about – a peaceful future for the child, than was afforded his father.

There are children and adults who learned to hurt, maim and kill here, often under the influence of drugs, for power or money. Some children lost their innocence too soon. Instead of playing with toys, they had live ammunition and the consequences that go with using it.

I inform these officers who have been so interesting and more caring than I could have hoped that I will put some of what I learned on paper. I will include photos that hopefully giving a small piece of insight into what is happening in Rio. There is so much more to write in a city as diverse as it is beautiful.

I am sad to say my goodbyes and warm hugs are exchanged. Their company has left me again with more lasting memories. There is always something heart-warming about feeling welcome or valuable in some way.

It helps keep my spirits up on those rare low days I like to keep at bay when the world seems a dark and hurtful place. Lieutenant Colonel Yunes has been a good friend and helpful to me on my travels in Rio. He has afforded me an opportunity to see this beautiful city and all the work that's ongoing behind its majestic scenery. Despite the bad, there is utter goodness. The evidence presents itself at every corner as people praise the efforts being made in their city, to make it safe. He is passionate and committed to making the lives of others even better and gives hope for the police of Rio.

We will stay in touch of course. It is easy to generalise people and their positions – but there is also the human side I have come to know and like. I make my own judgments and try not to listen to idle gossip. In my experience people who fight hard for an issue may appear cold and uncaring though the opposite may be true. To have these passionate feelings towards injustice, you must have sensitivity to the plight of others. Like most humans knowledge of pain no doubt will have been a strong teacher along the way. There may of course be a touch of 'kick ass' thrown in. Those I have known who tried to do their best in the face of strong opposition and tough circumstances, have a strong sense of justice.

My transport arrives and brings me back to my apartment in the Friday evening traffic. It's rush hour again like the world-over. Back home at my Rio apartment, there is not much time to prepare ahead of meeting my Danish friends again. Tonight is their final night in Rio. They are leaving at the weekend. Ulla and Henrik were so inclusive and kind as were their associates on this trip. It is nearing the time for me to go back to Ireland and recap on what I have seen and learned.

There was a reason for coming to Rio and I will keep a memory of it to be recalled as needed.

I ask Lieutenant Yunes if I can bring a number of the Danish delegation to Santa Marta favela, before they leave. A couple of them expressed a desire to see a more pacified favela. Hopefully in the morning this will be possible.

Copacabana/Lapa

I travel by taxi once again to Copacabana and this evening we will eat locally at a nearby restaurant that serves fish and meat dishes. It faces onto the sea and the glorious sea breeze blowing in on the patio-diners keeps us cool.

There are a lot of anecdotal stories told - some about surfing. There is another discussion about how the lives of those affected by drug and alcohol misuse directly or indirectly can be improved by the work being done in Greenland.

Projects that help people gain control of how they live and support them finding alternatives that help are needed more than ever. It is one way of showing we care. I've obtained the promised literature and DVD 'Working Lab Greenland'- explaining about the work involved in the social pedagogical theatre's methods and experiences on the island. It is about the work the Danish delegate Klaus is carrying out in Greenland and includes the concept of teaching through acting. This type of theatre is developed to work with and address social problems. It involves debate, public discussion and support in finding solutions. It is a very interesting piece of work and I find it fascinating that such projects are in operation in Greenland. I will take a closer look at this when I finish in Brasil.

In time of recession it is even more important to realise life goes on regardless. No point in wasting time on what we cannot change. Harnessing positive energy and working together, we will get through it all somewhat unscathed. Hopefully we will be a lot more grateful for what we do have. Dealing with problems day by day makes problems surmountable and being grateful will bring happiness to a dark day.

My Danish friends and I walk up the path onto the rocks where we can see skilled surfers catching the waves in the moonlight. They return surfing on the whitened crests of waves. Everyone is lost in thought as we look out to sea. The only sounds in the night are the high waves crashing onto the jagged rocks beside us spraying us with mist. We watch as they slide back into the dark depths below. There are a small number of people sitting up here, some drinking or with friends. I wouldn't come here alone but tonight is calm and I am with my other dinner companions.

I will be leaving soon with a more informed view of Rio. There is always that sadness in leaving friends behind. Van Gogh once said, 'The more I think it over, the more I feel that there is nothing more truly artistic than to love people'. Many spend the greatest part of their lives working without realising the richness in taking time for their friendships, relationships, friends and family.

The more I travel, the more I realise most memories and lessons come from people and not places. There are so many stories here that touch me - from the police who are trying to make a difference, little Janice surviving alone in this big city and those working long hours in cafes and shops earning a low income to provide for their families. Most of all it is the people of the favelas who hold my attention.

Their ability to overcome, grow and live regardless of the extreme conditions and adapt to changes, is in itself inspiring. Life goes on here. People do not waste time. Even hurtful pasts are being shed, to live in the present fully. A strategy I fully support.

The famous footballer Pelé is an example, coming from the slums, of how obstacles can be overcome to achieve the most incredible dreams. Growing communities, rich and poor, live side by side. The young men and women caught up needlessly in barbaric criminality make me question our ability to inflict this level of suffering on others.

A lot of suffering is preventable. People here want more from their politicians as they do in Ireland. This focus on Rio has provided the launching pad to air social problems, corruption and any biased media coverage. Help for the people of Rio is long overdue.

Ireland also is in the midst of great change in this economic recession. Ireland's citizens also deserve to have accountability, responsibility and care from those in positions of power lest we develop further problems. It is to be expected from those who are elected by the people or earned their fortune off their backs to provide this.

'Overcoming poverty is not humanity, it is an act of justice', Nelson Mandela

We take a taxi to Lapa to watch the business of the area as we sit and chat about Rio. I have confirmation another Santa Marta favela visit is possible in the morning. I agree to take Klaus and another delegate back with me to view it. They both have a genuine interest in viewing the longest pacified favela.

24th November - Santa Marta Favela 2nd Visit

Police allow me to bring the delegation to the favela on my own. The UPP police will meet me at the top of the favela on arrival. We walk to the favela entrance where some local residents are standing. They recognize me from the previous visit to the favela. Like I said, the locals here are used to their community in the shanty houses and know when strangers arrive. We discuss their involvement in setting up a guided tour for visitors. This is an initiative coming from the residents of the Santa Marta favela itself. Already they are taking a pride in their pacified community. People here are now in a position to utilise this new way of life in order to bring posterity. They are becoming more organised and are wearing t-shirts, imprinted with the name of the favela. Before pacification this was not something anyone wanted to do. The locals are now taking control of their environment and want to maintain the status quo.

The three of us step into the large-windowed lift that takes us up the steep climb, past a number of stop off points, to the top. There are local people and children, some seated, others standing, beside us as we slowly trundle up the hill in the heat. The higher we climb, the more amazing the view.

It is very hot and I make my way to the police base as arranged where I collect my supply of water.

Three UPP police accompany us through the favela. They are shy at first to speak English but eventually use whatever words they know. I do likewise in Portuguese. One tells me he is a Black belt in Jujitsu and teaches it in the city. Many police here are trained in some form of martial arts.

It is common for police to have two jobs, as salaries are not so high. Many are young men or women some married with families. We visit a large building where they are preparing for a concert. It reminds me of a jazz club with large black portrait pictures hanging from the walls. There is a lot of community activity in this favela and free classes are available. My travelling companions are amazed at the layout of the favela, the view, narrow paths, steep steps and tiny houses clamouring for space. Interesting to see their reaction to the stories of its more criminal past and the change they now see.

The buildings at the square are painted in bright colours. I am told the window with the shutter pushed open upwards, overlooking the exit from the favela, had other uses. When the criminals were in power, snipers sat at the window where they had easy opportunity to shoot unwanted visitors. Bullet holes are visible in the walls. It wears the marks of the wanton violence that took place here. Just four years ago this was a community involved in urban warfare and under the rule of drug gangs and criminals.

We are nearing the end of our walk now. I see an older woman sitting in the shade, flanked by men in their late 30s on either side. I notice an unusual tattoo on one shirtless man's arm. I have to speak with them. I ask if I can take a photo of the tattoo but the woman says no in Portuguese.

The two men are her sons who give me permission to take the photograph. However, I decline in respect of their mother's wishes. After asking my name, the mother tells me hers, shakes my hand and agrees to a photograph of the tattoo. It depicts a vicious dog with blood dripping from its teeth. The man proudly shows off this image, spread across his upper arm. It depicts the threat of being ripped and torn apart.

These are memories of bygone days when the possibility of a savage death hung in the favela's air. Before pacification between rival drug gangs, it was 'dog eat dog' if you wanted to survive. It's a very descriptive tattoo and I thank them for allowing me to take the photo. A man nearby has small stab wounds on his body another way of remembering the previous gang violence no longer part of daily living here.

Klaus and his friend have been asking plenty of questions. He has seen shantytowns in South Africa and is no stranger to what poverty can bring. This has been an interesting experience for the Danish delegates seeing at first hand Santa Marta favela. A lady, in a tour t-shirt approaches and offers to arrange a return visit for us. We take her contact details though I have my own liaison personnel.

When the weight of emotional pain, poverty and cruel abandonment is left on people's shoulders it is difficult to rise without help. As I have seen working with drug problems if you keep doing the same thing you get the same results. Make a change. Time to leave and we say our goodbyes again to our accompanying police. They have been great company on our trek through the favela, helpful, caring and informative. Down in the lift once more with one of the nicest views of any descent.

My companions thank me for helping to arrange the visit, which they thoroughly enjoyed. I was hoping they would get the same feeling of amazement and wonder I had - and they did. One of the men asks me to show him where the gift shops are in Rio; he wants to buy some presents for his family. I wait at my usual restaurant while he shops and reflect on all the information I have acquired on this trip. My new Danish friends have added to the trip with a kinship for my work.

I hadn't thought to meet too many Europeans on my travels here. Having spent a lot of time in Sweden, meeting people from neighbouring Denmark feels familiar. I am grateful to find others who see the benefit of working with and reducing drug and alcohol problems. It's agreed alleviating poverty is part of the solution. It's nice to sit here and relax. No appointments to make, no social events to prepare for.

I get encouragement from the conversation at this small cafe. The general consensus is that help is needed here to help many people suffering from addiction, ill health and poverty. I see it here in Rio the change that starts when people no longer stand by and watch but become active in whatever way they can to help. Every person who lives, works and invests here has a responsibility to get involved.

Ireland has growing problems with drugs and related murders. Once again man's inhumanity to man. I live on an island where young people die on a regular basis from drugs, alcohol misuse, suicide and murder. There is increased criminal activity, organised crime, gangs, weapons, reduced policing and a feeling of hopelessness.

Does anyone care out there? Does anyone in powerful positions have a plan and know how to execute it to resolve the mounting social issues? Has anyone the courage to stand out and be counted? It is necessary to change a national drug policy that has seen a consistent rise in drug use and the fall out. – It's an abysmal failure.

Ireland has great and famous people the world over known

for their entrepreneurism.

Ireland's physical natural beauty is recognized globally. People fought and died in the past to gain freedom in the Republic of Ireland for this parcel of land in the Atlantic. It is sad to say it now appears it is being handed over to enslavement of another kind –drugs and alcohol. The drug lords are ruling their chosen territories. Evictions in Ireland, a dark reminder of its tortured past, one we never thought could happen again are back with a bang. There is no one else to blame but our own for the crimes and inhumanities to families.

Investors

I realise from my visit and further investigations that there are major international investors interested in Brasil. Oil is one of its resources and it's a commodity never ignored by big global players. There are others willing to invest in the telecommunications industry. There is the potential to make billions of Euros or US dollars in returns here. The question is how will Brasilian people and Rio benefit from this? Will money become available to pay for the resources they need, especially for people in poverty? I really hope so.

Some fear that a lure of money to be made in Brasil may give rise to increased corruption. One billionaire George Soros, already an investor in Brasil, has an interest in the legalisation of cannabis/marijuana. He is a board member in one of the most active organisations trying to achieve that goal. Richard Branson and Sting are also members of its international honourary board. That organisation also gives grants to other organisations working for reform according to their grant giving criteria. He is a very strategic investor. So far he has invested substantially in Brasil.

A number of Latin American countries are talking about drug law reform from the present illegal stand. There are proposals to legitimise the production, sale and consumption of cannabis (marijuana) in Uruguay. Anyone over eighteen will be able to buy 40 grams of cannabis under the newly proposed drug law for Uruguay. So the obvious black market will focus on the under eighteens. Uruguay is now being called the 'laboratory' where keen eyes internationally will view the effects of legalisation.

The organisation Soros is involved in claims it "has been deeply involved in these unfolding events since the onset, advising leaders and high-level officials in Latin America, providing them with research and information to support their proposals, and appearing in dozens of US and Latin American media outlets to contextualize these developments." It will be interesting to see what supporting research is given by the organisation. Internationally there is also a vast body of very credible evidence refuting the benefit of legalising drugs. I have met and worked with many genuine and capable people in this field, who have tirelessly investigated the effects of legalisation. They will in no way support this move from what they have learned over the years. Nor do I for that matter.

Everyone knows the old plan is that if you can get one drug legalised under any guise, the other drugs may follow with the same reasoning.

There are people waiting to patent the drugs in order to sell them if they can get them distributed legally.

Governments may get the tax from the sales but they will need it as the rise in use affects badly every person, community and service in their country. People should not be hoodwinked into believing this is in some way for the benefit of communities. Nor is it that the drug cartels will give up this lucrative business if made legal. It's for greed and money - pure and simple.

Soros is better known for his insider trader conviction under France's insider trading laws. Soros was also nicknamed 'the man who broke the Bank of England' referring to his currency speculation with the UK sterling in 1992, that reputedly earned him over 1billion sterling pounds which caused serious problems for sterling at the time. He makes money but at what expense to people?

It shows the measure of a man when you see how an insatiable appetite for money gives him more than he can spend in numerous lifetimes. Soros has in recent times invested millions of US dollars in Brasil's tele-communications especially in São Paulo. It is reported he has also invested in Brasilian oil. Soros supports legalising drugs. Training courses for journalists and media are another venture being supported. This is a worrying trend. What can be gained by influencing media? It is good to remember the old saying; 'the pen is mightier than the sword.' Soros support for legalisation is happening in other countries too. Representatives from a variety of social positions, community, church and professional representatives discussing the further aim of legalising drugs are usually brought together. A conference was held in Rio de Janeiro with professional and community representatives that presented legalisation as the way to go.

Vigilance will be needed if Brasil is to navigate towards a just and fair economic and social platform for the future. In a book written by Soros, he says if it was up to him he would legalise all drugs except the dangerous ones like crack cocaine. Legalising drugs can never become socially acceptable because of the pain and suffering that follow as a result of their increased use. Alcohol is legal and is one of the most misused drugs in the world. When Head shops sold herbal drugs before they too were criminalised in Ireland, I saw an unprecedented rise in teenagers using and addicted to these

substances. The users said to me that if it is legal they assume it must be safe to use otherwise why adults would legalise such drugs. Substances sold as bath salts and other herbs when tested showed up as pretty much the same as cocaine, marijuana/cannabis, amphetamines and other addictive substances. People in Brasil have come through so much that now is not the time to go back to slavery. Drugs enslave the mind, body and spirit and affect everyone around the user.

Drugs are not dangerous because they are illegal. They are illegal because they are dangerous.

Contrary to Soros's views on controlling drugs through legalisation, the opposite has proved more effective in countries such as Sweden. Back in the 1980's they decriminalised' some drugs. Millions of doses of amphetamines were made available, cannabis was decriminalised and methadone was distributed and the result was a dramatic rise in drug use and addiction. It was the ordinary people of Sweden who demanded the National policy change and thus began Sweden's successful reign as having one of the lowest rates of drug use in Europe. This was achieved under a restrictive policy on drugs not liberal. It also is recognised as having one of the best social care systems in the world.

Unfortunately this success makes them a thorn in the side of the legalisation movement. Pressure is now being diverted to get Sweden to capitulate and follow the other sheep that have invested in policies that have seen increased drug use.

In Rio, the work of the BOPE and UPP police are showing more positive results in reclaiming favelas from drugs gangs. The illegality of these substances gives the police power to intervene and the results are not lost on me or indeed the favela communities. I think it best to follow the Police plan rather than Soros. I muse over the relevance of his name, 'Soros'.

I feel the need to highlight the threat of drugs to Rio and why people remain aware of how some wealthy investors may have other agendas for profit. I have yet to see, in all my years working in this field, any illicit substances that are not dangerous in some way. I recall all the young people who have died as a result of so called 'recreational' drug use. I keep many of their obituary photos so I remember they are not just statistics but real people who leave families behind. Approximately half of all suicides in Ireland are drugs or alcohol related. Rising crime and the link to drugs is a frightening trend for this island. Drug money has corrupted many organisations and political representatives worldwide.

Rio, like Ireland is entitled to have responsible, law- abiding people at the helm to improve people's lives and make sure all relevant social supports are in place. At a time of great wealth is a great opportunity to do just that. Ireland, I believe, squandered its chance to make a difference when resources were flowing during the so-called Celtic Tiger years.

During that period, I saw a greater increase in drug use as out-dated strategies proved ineffective - coupled with a growing demand for drugs from those with more money to splash out on quick fixes.

Inadequate numbers of prevention, intervention and drug free recovery programmes assist the epidemic level of drug and alcohol misuse in Ireland.

There is a new vocabulary that makes drug use sound safe. Those with a greedy agenda encourage the inaccurate and manipulative use of words. Its purpose is to misguide people about the risk involved in all drug use. Perversely misguiding people has the effect of encouraging drug use, making money and disregarding the cost to society. 'Safe use,' 'soft drugs', recreational use' and 'medical use' fool people into believing certain drugs are harmless - some can actually help certain illnesses but they don't give all the facts. It may be one chemical of the four hundred in the drug that may or may not be useful. There is no such thing as 'safe' use, just drug use. I sat at a conference for legalisation, biting my tongue while I listened to plans that would generate a lot of money.

People living in the favelas know exactly what it means to have drug use in their midst and have seen the results up close. Parents have watched their children's behaviour change to destructive. Over time it was the drug gangs who took over the poorer areas of Rio. Now it will also be a challenge to prevent unscrupulous investors. Those who may want to pay their way into Rio's elite to manipulate for personal benefit, with disregard for its population, are not welcome. It is important the people of Rio and Brasil once more are not caught in the business of money, corruption and drugs.

We all like to think we are different and problems happen everywhere else and not on our doorsteps...until it happen to us!

This is not about a geographical location but how we live, care for those most vulnerable and put the necessary resources into the areas that make the most difference. Weeding out corruption at all levels; especially when it invades corridors of power is high on the list.

Money Laundering & Banks

There are some Banks who have dirtied their hands laundering drug money for criminal drug cartels and terrorism. These banks were formerly seen as playing a pivotal role in society and oh how the mighty have fallen low. Like I said money off the backs of misery and death is nothing to be proud of or respected. There is nothing clever in making money this way. Some Banks in Europe laundered over 360 billion euro of Mexican and Colombian Drug cartels drug money from 2006 to 2010.

The US Senate Committee on Homeland Security and Governmental Affairs issued a 339-page report in July 2012, which detailed the list of "criminal" behaviour, by London based HSBC bank. The report covered how the bank washed over $881 million through its US unit, for the Mexican Sinaloa Cartel and for the Norte del Valle Cartel in Colombia. The bank was also seen to have violated US sanctions relating to banking with Iran, Libya, Cuba, Burma, and Sudan. Some sanctions are in connection with terrorism.

The United States Intelligence Community considers the Sinaloa Cartel "the most powerful drug trafficking organization in the world"

The Sinaloa cartel originates from a region that is a major producer of opium and marijuana. Heroin comes from opium. The Sinaloa drug cartel is cited as bringing over 200 tons of cocaine and large amounts of heroin into America, where it was distributed, between the 1990s and 2008, according to the US Attorney General. One of Sinaloa's territories is the Mexican/Arizona border into the US, where illegal immigrants are sometimes forced into the drug gangs.

Forty nine headless bodies were found dumped in Northern Mexico along the roadside. Hands, feet and the heads had been chopped off. Even more frightening is that no bullet wounds were seen suggesting the dismembering happened before death according to police in a report. Mutilation to the upper and lower body was another factor on the men and women found. This was the third massacre in recent times as the war between Sinaloa and Zelas drug cartels in the infamous region known as the 'Triangle of Death' continues according to these reports. The HSBC bank was accused of not monitoring over $670 billion in wire transfers and in excess of $9.4 billion purchases of U.S. currency from HSBC Mexico. This allowed Mexican cartel monies to be laundered or cleaned, according to prosecutors in the case. HSBC also violated U.S. economic sanctions that are in place against Libya, Iran, Burma, Sudan and Cuba. This information was also filed in the case against the bank. HSBC is Europe's largest bank and will pay $1.25 billion forfeits and $665 million in civil penalties as part of an agreed settlement. Unfortunately this agreement avoids any other criminal proceedings about the charges made.

US Senator Elizabeth Warren questioned officials from the Treasury Department as to what would it take before criminal charges would be brought against banks involved in such activities? Warren went on to note how people are most likely jailed for drug possession, not minimizing the act, rather highlighting how laundering the spoils through banks did not incur such penalties. The senator went on to say, 'if you're caught with an ounce of cocaine, the chances are good you're going to go to jail... But evidently, if you launder nearly a billion dollars for drug cartels and violate our international sanctions, your company pays a fine and you go home and sleep in your own bed at night.'

Ordinary people are being brought to court over payments they cannot make as part of the economic downturn; much of this is to banks. Families have been evicted from their homes in Ireland. Yet none of the bank bosses involved in money laundering have gone to jail for the most heinous of crimes, as I see it. What can be worse than inadequately monitoring money transfers which inadvertently help keep large scale murdering drug cartels in operation? Laundering drug money is one of the worst crimes imaginable. This money is the proceeds from the sale of death and destruction in the form of drugs, used by young people in our communities. It is ludicrous and unjust. Buying the drugs is another way of lining their pockets I must add lest we forget our responsibilities. As for legalisation, do it and they will legitimately sell the drugs – no surprise! Pardon the pun but they will be laughing all the way to the bank. Cartels will not relinquish their power and greed through legalisation. In fact from what I have learned they would love it.

The Wachovia bank in the US was heavily involved in money laundering moving up to $378.4 billion over several years. It made a deal to pay fines of 160 million dollars and get a 'deferred prosecution' agreement in place. Wachovia is not the only bank, there are others allegedly involved in the same business. Banks it appears is where the money can be in the global market of drugs they say. If banks did not clean the dirty money for drug cartels, it would make life very difficult for them and not so easy to function. There is a tendency to pay fines but this I believe will not stem the growth of illegal laundering unless the relevant bankers are brought to court.

It is easy to look at the drug users along the streets and blame them for the state of the country and ostracise them. This is while taking our eye off the ball where the main action is actually happening. Like I said no banker was prosecuted and imprisoned for illegal involvement in the drugs trade in the US to date. Reducing laundering possibilities reduces opportunities for the cartels to function.

It is about not accepting the unacceptable. A friend of mine once told me that when he started his career, he was idealistic and believed he could make a difference. I am sure he has, but watching the corruption that takes place in positions of power can put a serious dent in idealism. Nevertheless we still need those who believe it is worth making the effort.

Change

The visionaries of possibilities are those who understand that change stems from one person. One person can start a domino effect – one drop of water is the beginning of a river. Rosa Parks's act of defiance and the Montgomery Bus Boycott in the USA is testament to that. Taking her seat on a bus one day, where black people were not allowed, was the start of the American Civil Rights Movement. Never underestimate the power of the ordinary person. A peaceful action – no violence involved.

'If you think you are too small to make a difference, try sleeping with a mosquito.' - Dali Lama XIV.

Rio has now an opportunity to start something new. Do I believe it is possible? I most certainly do especially after what I've witnessed on this visit to Rio. The evidence is easy to see and hear. People feel Rio is becoming a safer place and the effects of the policing strategies are without doubt welcome here. Follow up and a continuation of care will make this project viable in the long term.

I'm beginning to think Ireland could learn from Rio. At a time when the drug culture gains hold of Irish society, Rio is regaining its worth, its personality and its power from the drug lords. It is a difficult process where even the simplest and peaceful of public demonstrations can be hijacked for other motives.

Action now means a new start in Rio.

Rio for the World cup and Olympics will have different meanings for different people. Many will come as spectators, to support and to enjoy the fun and the sport. Some will come to profiteer from drug peddling, ticket touting and crime.

Those making money from the drugs and arms trade will always try to undermine efforts for peace. Peace is not in their best interest! It's bad for business! However the residents of Rio, who have emerged from a life of fear and threat can hold their head high and proudly celebrate the events alongside all others. They have broken records and scored hat- tricks in their own feats against abuse. Those who were forced to sell drugs or steal, were beaten, tortured and burned. Those who stand up to the crime lords - they are the ones who deserve the gold medals. I am forever hopeful for their future.

Rio de Janeiro in English 'January River' is one of the most fascinating and beautiful regions to visit. I have no hesitation in returning. People are living out their daily normal lives in this city. Some come to visit and decide to stay. My overriding impression that I take away is the warmth of its people in a variety of ways in a geographical setting difficult to surpass. As for having events of great magnitude, Rio does it like no other. One million attendees at the Copacabana parade didn't break a sweat on their brow.

I'm looking forward to the great sporting events. Roll on Rio.

Rio de Janeiro (January River)

'The river got to keep on flowing where the force of nature takes it' unknown.

FOLLOWING ON

Since my visit to Rio de Janeiro 36 favelas have now been pacified with more to follow.

Rio has indeed successfully hosted the Pope's visit drawing the expected influx of people to the region. The new Pope openly met the crowds and left unscathed as the Colonel predicted. Rio has experienced citizens marching in the streets to voice their need for more Government support to address poverty and social issues. They no longer wish to accept that their basic human rights are ignored. People want help and now it appears is their time to voice their wishes.

Sadly Uruguay capitulated and has taken the road to legalisation of cannabis, a decision they will regret. It will haunt them into the future I have no doubt. Like Holland when it decriminalised the use of cannabis in some 'coffee shops' Uruguay will attract drug tourism. It will be interesting how they cope with the effects of drugs on visitors and its own population as use of the substances rises bringing with it addiction. Drugs are addictive and that alone will create a growing market for the suppliers. They can't lose now. It will be a long time before this lucrative business relying on people's compulsion for drugs when addicted, will be allowed to abate. Rescheduling and making cannabis illegal once more will have to happen. It is a sad day for Uruguay and its children.

According to polls 63% opposed the bill and only 26% approved it. Nevertheless despite the lack of support from the people, the bill was passed by the Chamber of Deputies and ratified by the senate and finally signed by President Mujica. President José Mujica met with billionaire and philanthropist George Soros, at the end of 2013.

The billionaire supports the changes in drug laws. Soros has offered funding to evaluate the impact of the law.

It is healthier if independent monitors review the results of legalising cannabis. They must not have a vested interest or benefit in any way from its sale or legalisation. Otherwise there is a conflict of interest should this not be the case. Too much is at stake globally – as other countries consider their options.

Recently at the United Nations General Assembly a great deal of focus was given to global drug policy reform with Guatemala, México, and even Colombia calling for major changes.

These countries have been home to some of the most notorious and brutal drug cartels known to man. The fact they want the possible legalisation of drugs, makes it questionable that the drug cartels who rule, do not stand to lose their empires from such an act. Most certainly they will benefit. As I said before their interest lies in money, power and greed without conscience.

In the meantime the Obama administration in the US has said it would not counteract Colorado's and Washington's legalisation of marijuana. Some outlets sell marijuana under the label of medical use already and there has been problems with this move. Concerned parents and communities have lobbied long and hard against changes in laws that would legalise marijuana. Marijuana is still illegal in the 50 states under the federal government. Going even further the Treasury department has developed new guidelines that could allow for Banks to do business with and handle monies from marijuana dispensers. Protests to these moves have come from people concerned at the liberal availability of marijuana.

They question the implications and possible fall out when banks legally get to handle legitimate drug money. What can of worms will it open? Since the economic crisis many people have lost trust with some financial institutions as corruption unfolds. Since marijuana became more easily accessible there is a 30% increase in children presenting at Emergency hospital units where they have mistakenly ingested the substance. It's now sold in a variety of marketable packages – in the form of sweets is one such method.

Senator Chuck Grassley (R-Iowa), a ranking member of the Senate Judiciary Committee made a statement, "Marijuana trafficking is illegal under federal law, and it's illegal for banks to deal with marijuana sale proceeds under federal law. Only Congress can change these laws. The administration can't change the law with a memo."

It is curious to see how Obama's administration adheres to federal laws. George Soros, mentioned earlier, has long been seen as a supporter of President Obama – during his election and re-election as President. Soros made donations to these campaigns. He can afford to donate millions into his chosen areas of interest. It will be interesting to see what legacy remains following the present decisions in the US and for its people.

The scourge of gangs in Brasil is still being targeted as an ex footballer in Rio was beheaded by criminals. His satchel containing his head was found on the doorstep of his home by his wife, in the morning. The reason for his gruesome death is being investigated. Sadly the famous footballer Pele, has seen his son sentenced to 33 years in prison for drug money laundering – he is to appeal it.

In Ireland we have seen the dismembered body of a male discarded in a field. It was suggested according to reports that he was involved to some degree in the drug trade.

His family wept as they asked for his head to be returned. It was located some time later. Numerous women and men are unaccounted for and remain on the missing persons list in Ireland. Some it is thought have been murdered but their bodies have not come to light.

In the Phoenix Park in Dublin Gardaí (police) seeing a small fire burning, investigated. It was a sleeping bag containing the body of a man who was set alight by another. The deceased man had also sustained head injuries.

Shootings and drug gang rivalry continues in Ireland too. Drive by shootings and gangland style executions are more common. The attempted murders of gangland members – saved by bullet-proof vests in the past was viewed on American movies – now it is for real in Ireland. Gardaí (police) have made major seizures of drugs – some gangs have international links. Following the resignation of the Garda Commissioner the first female Garda Commissioner is in charge for the interim but hopefully long term. A good worker in the field Commissioner Noirin O Sullivan is well respected. I hope she is given the support she needs to do her job effectively - commitment to doing her best will not be a problem for this woman I know.

Suicides sadly still continue. It's a blight on Irish families and communities – pain and suffering for all concerned – lack of hope - some choose to end it all.

It is nice to think Rio over there has all the problems. Anyone looking at the island of Ireland and its reported crimes and suffering may be forgiven for wondering about visiting here. Tourism needs to thrive if we want to help Ireland back on to its feet during the economic recession.

Irish people overall want to do the right thing and live happily. They want to see families grow up safely and not in the drug culture, drug gangs and crimes. Sounds like the favela parents when you think about it. Nevertheless in Ireland we do have one of the highest rates of drug use in Europe consistently. It is an embarrassment that we repeat strategies that are not reducing the phenomenal rise in violent criminality. Drug and addiction related suffering prospers at the expense of happiness. Denial of our situation remains high it seems. When people are scared to go out alone, worry about robberies, physical attacks, murder, child safety, lack of adequate social care support or poverty then something is malfunctioning. We do have a problem and a big one at that. I hope we can get the courage in Ireland to alter our attitudes, invest the necessary resources and reverse this trend. I know we can do it when we unite and work together for the greater good. Taking care of each other is vital to sustain wellbeing. We are but segments making up the whole. What happens to one affects us all.

Yes I learned a lot from Rio. I learned how any country can develop the same problems as it has over the years left unchecked. I also know how continuing to safeguard this wonderful and dynamic city is the right and just thing to do. It is working. As I said at the outset, that is exciting.
The people of Ireland have the power to turn this social decline around. Political interest will further dramatically shift the balance. Must we have major sporting fixture before we clean up our problems? I hope not! I note there is talk of such an event. Do we have to wait? I don't believe so - the time to act is now.

Speaking of achievements and to bring you up to date about the health of my friend Alex - he has miraculously survived his major health problems. He now stands 6' 4" as his two new prosthesis legs have added an inch or two. Alex plans on getting back into his martial arts. Already he is taking magnificent photos with even more joy, enthusiasm and light that he includes in all his work. His positive attitude, gratitude to his loving relationships and what matters in life is enlightening. Alex's perseverance and love of life is infectious. Wasting time and waiting for 'the right time' to live and love is not on his list. Alex is doing it now. He represents how Rio de Janeiro steps up when the going gets tough.

Alex has kindly given me a number of his photos for

inclusion so I can show where he has travelled from in his recovery to where he is now. Everything begins with one step. Another man's journey and one we can all learn from. Obrigada Alex.

The answer to our problems lies within us. Human beings are very resilient and come back from the most extraordinary situations. They learn to move forward. We never know how much we can achieve until we try. Viva Rio.

72. New football ground in Rocinha.
73. Boy in polo top in favela Rocinha.
74. Woman repairs clothes in favela
75. Proud wearer of the Rocinha favela football team jersey.
76. Former drug dealing den now a community/sports area.
77. Iced fruit mixture shop.

198

78. Receiving PMERJ police unit shield from Captain Lima - Police Academy
79. PMERJ police arm shield. 80. Police sing 'Brasilia' for my visit..
81. Police Academy training. 82. Major Robson & colleagues following recruit training in the rain . 83. Police Academy Rio   84. Academy - Colonel, trainee officers & me after their presentation

85

6

87

8

90

85. Beach toys - beer can and green coco cost nothing
86. Rio de Janeiro City Centre
87. Holiday weekend smiles.
88. Little girl smiling
89. Parents bad hair day
90. Mountain climbing at Sugar Loaf

200

91. Dark Angel.   92. Onlookers at Gay Pride Parade.
93. Dressing Up.   94. Watchful eye   95. 2 smoking barrels, reminders.
96. Gay Pride Parade visitors   97. On duty at parade, all goes well.

98. Flag lowering naval base at Sugar Loaf
Mountain 99. I promise I won't stand upon
the wall 100. Janice relaxed. Rio 101.
'Working girls' & Janice . 102. Klaus Rubin,
member of Danish delegation, & Marie
Byrne - amusing stories time
103. Rio de Janeiro from Sugar Loaf
Mountain. 104. Ulla Diderichsen &
Henrik Bjørn-Jepsen Danish delegates

In Santa Marta favela

Happier Days in Santa Marta favela – Bright colours

105. Carioca aqueduct (Lapa)
106. New football ground,Santa Marta favela, more
gruesome body parts kicked here in the past
107. Shanty Town living
108. Clothes drying.
109. Michael Jackson filmed video here
110. With Ten Gabriele (UPP) at Michael Jackson statue
111. With Danish delegate Ulla Diderichsen at Ipanema,
conference reception

112

113

114

115

112. Mini Mouse in favela, happier times now
113. Santa Marta favela, helper
114. Painting favela, like Michael Jackson
115. Former 'sniper's' window.
116. 'The Civil war in Rio' how it was

206

117. Alex following his legs amputations (photo Alex Rodrigues)
118. Elaine - PMERJ police - a great help
119. Alex taking new steps in recovery/ Face forward (Photo by Alex Rodrigues)
120. City centre architecture

Policing

There are now 36 UPP pacification police bases established in favelas in Rio de Janeiro and crime levels continue to decrease. There are approximately 8,592 police officers now involved in the Pacification units (UPP police). There are said to be ten UPP police units still working out of containers, awaiting permanent bases to be built. Another problem cited in reports in recent times for the UPP police units, is police car maintenance. Approximately 38 cars are said to be out of action. A company previously lent its support to up keeping the cars. Due to financial problems this service has now stopped.

Police behaviour continues to be monitored to detect any possible wrongdoings. On the other side sadly a number of police have been killed in the line of duty. Thirty year-old Fabiana Aparecida de Souza, who had only been on the force a few months, was the first police officer to die in an occupied favela. She was in a UPP police station in the Nova Brasília area of the Complexo do Alemão when she was shot. The building was fired upon by a number of attackers - Fabiana was hit in the abdomen by a rifle bullet.
A second female police officer Alda Rafael Castillo, 26, was shot in the back on Sunday the 4th of February 2014, in a separate incident. This murder took place during an attack on a police base once again. She died of her injuries later in hospital. Alda, according to officials was a member of the military police since 2012 and studying psychology. Two people standing nearby and another police officer were wounded in this attack.

Weapons, including an AK-47 and drug packaging equipment were found during subsequent raids according to investigators. These deaths show the vulnerability of those police who try to serve communities honestly in order to bring stability to the region. The risk of death is always present. There appears to be few outcries in relation to police deaths in the line of duty.

There are still police who, as I said, try to protect and serve with their lives. The favela Complexo do Alemão continues to present problems and further focus will now be given to rid this favela of criminal rule. The 'Black Blocs' criminal gang deliberately launched a rocket over a cameraman from TV Bandeirantes. The reporter, Santiago Andrade, 49, is in serious condition following a major head injury to his skull at this time.

The need for consistent investment, resources, and community support in all the favelas and local areas must continue so that the improvements that have begun will continue.

Two more UPP (Pacifying Police Unit) officers were killed; Rodrigo de Souza Paes Leme and Wagner Viera da Costa were killed in the Complexo do Alemão and Complexo da Penha, both Zona Norte (North Zone) of Rio. Social issues and policing continue to need massive resources if they are to counteract the problems grown over many years. Patience, investment, consistency, time and working together can I believe affect change

The problems grew over many years - it is obvious the UPP police projects must be given time to unite with residents in order to combat the residue from past corruption on any side.

Major parliamentary support for police counteracting the emergence of violence - Rio's citizens who need further substantial social care services and human rights issues must now be prioritised. Action is required, not weak promises to satisfy global questions. People are tired of their enduring struggles - equal rights and fair treatment is what they now need. Honest men and women who care deeply for Rio's people placed at the helm of the political structure will help these great people grow to their full potential. It is starting now as recognition of their worth and needs become more apparent as they join in one voice in order to be heard.

'Don't give up just because of what someone said. Use that as motivation to push harder.' Anon.

A police battalion has been specially created to help control any possible demonstrations that may take place during the upcoming World Cup. It will also be involved at other large sporting and cultural events held in public venues, according to Rio de Janeiro state government.

Lieutenant Colonel Cândido Joseli continues as commander of the Battalion dealing with all the famous tourist sites and more in Rio – a wealth of experience on guard.

On the football front, teams taking part in the World Cup have the famous BOPE Police protection, in Rio. They protect with their lives so I know their expertise and commitment is always focused. Any upcoming World events in Rio will be worth viewing. In reverence to the efforts being made to safeguard Rio it is important the rest of the world focuses on what they are doing right. As with humans noting good behaviour will encourage more of the same.

My old friend Lieutenant Yunes is currently magistrate for the police of Rio de Janeiro. His dedication and work as part of the safeguarding of Rio de Janeiro continues. Rio is on the up and a feeling of hope permeates the streets of this beautiful city and its warm-hearted people. The sound of 'lights and action,' will hopefully signify change and not the beginning of a fictional movie. To see their dream of peace, happiness and equality reign in their homes is the best that globally we can ask for in their names. Being welcomed into the arms of Rio has left a lasting memory.

Quote by Brasilian Poet Paulo Coelho.

Someone that passed by us indeed will never leave completely for they will always leave something with us and will also take along something of us.

GLOSSARY

PMERJ (POLICE)

The Military Police of Rio de Janeiro State (Portuguese: Polícia Militar do Estado do Rio de Janeiro) (PMERJ) like other military polices in Brazil is a reserve and ancillary force of the Brazilian Army, and part of the System of Public Security and Brazilian Social Protection. Its members are called "State Military" person. The primary mission of PMERJ is ostensibly preventive policing for the maintenance of public order in the State of Rio de Janeiro.

UPP (Police)

The Pacifying Police Unit (Portuguese: Unidade de Polícia Pacificadora, also translated as Police Pacification Unit), abbreviated UPP, is a law enforcement and social services program pioneered in the state of Rio de Janeiro, Brazil, which aims at reclaiming territories, more commonly favelas, controlled by gangs of drug dealers. The program was created and implemented by State Public Security Secretary José Mariano Beltrame, with the backing of Rio Governor Sérgio Cabral. The stated goal of Rio's government is to install 40 UPPs by 2014.

CHOQUE BATTALION

The Choque battalion of Special Forces - Choque is a military police organization of the Military Police of Rio de Janeiro. The focus is to control riots and civil disturbances in open and closed areas to safeguard people, among other activities.

BOPE (Police)

Batalhão de Operações Policiais Especiais (BOPE) Special
Police Operations Battalion) is a Special Forces unit of the
Military Police of Rio de Janeiro State, Brazil.

Due to the nature of crime in favelas, BOPE units have
extensive experience in urban warfare as well as progression
in confined and restricted environments. It also utilises
equipment deemed more powerful than traditional civilian
law enforcement.

FAVELA

Favela is the name given to a slum or shanty-town in Rio de
Janeiro

Comando Vermelho

(Portuguese for Red Command) is a Brasilian politico
criminal organisation.